MW01449638

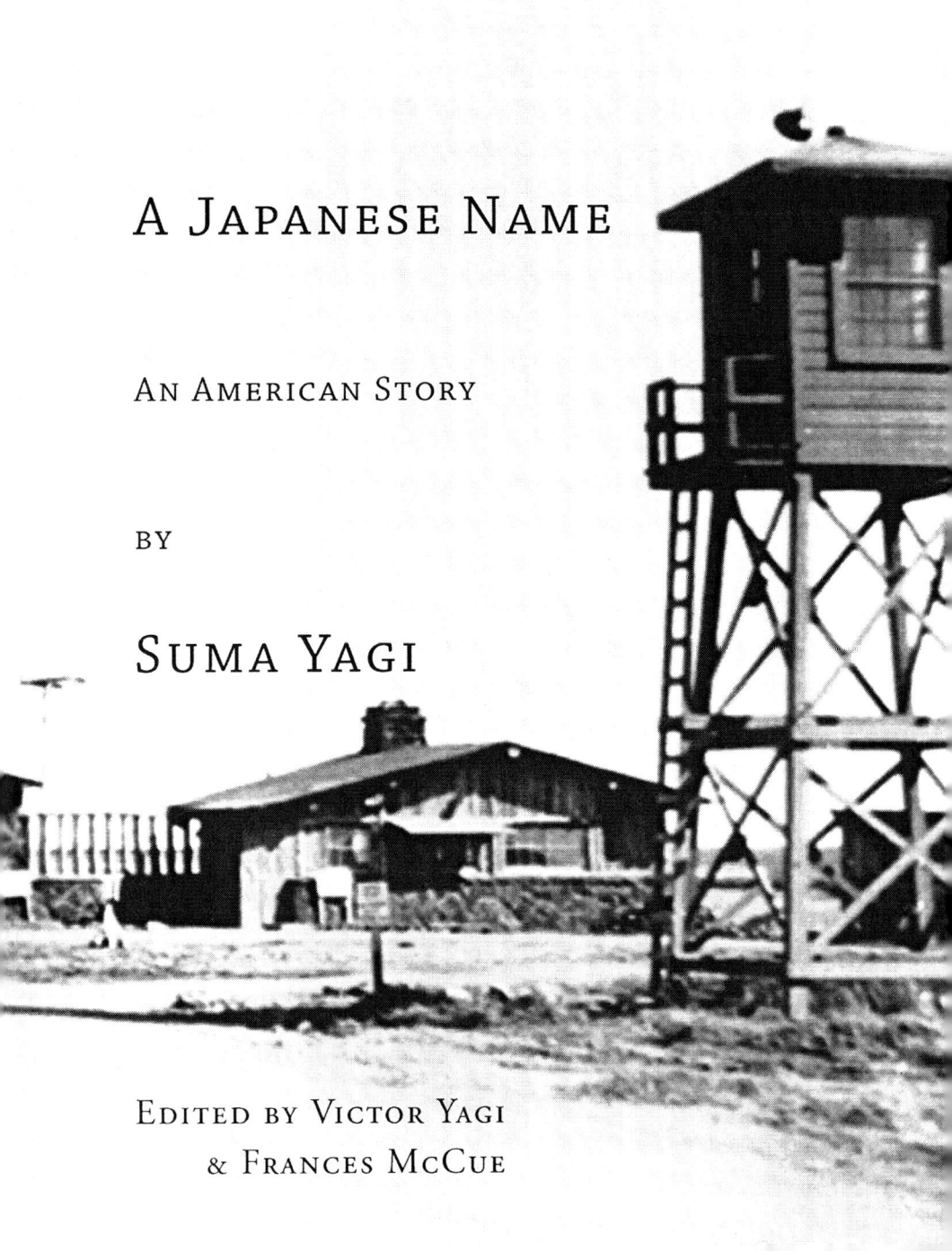

A Japanese Name

An American Story

by

Suma Yagi

Edited by Victor Yagi
& Frances McCue

'A Japanese Name' copyright © 2016 by Suma Yagi
All rights reserved.

No part of this book may be reproduced in any form or by any electronic or mechanical means, including information storage and retrieval systems, without permission in writing from the publisher, except by a reviewer, who may quote brief passages.

Interior photographs, unless otherwise noted, © 2016 the Yagi family.

Cover Images: Entrance to the Minidoka concentration camp, aka "Relocation Center," superimposed with an image of first grade students saying the Pledge of Allegiance. Photos courtesy of Densho: The Japanese American Legacy Project

Cover and book design: Vladimir Verano Third Place Press

Published by

Victor Yagi
victoryagi@gmail.com

ISBN: 978-0-9970550-0-9

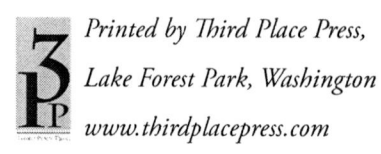

Printed by Third Place Press,
Lake Forest Park, Washington
www.thirdplacepress.com

Overleaf: Entrance to the Minidoka concentration camp, showing the guard tower and administration buildings.
Photo courtesy of Densho: The Japanese American Legacy Project

*To the memory of my parents
Harutoshi and Murako,
in honor of my children
Roberta, Martin, Victor and Teresa,
and to the future of my grandchildren,
Rachel, Ryan, Brandon, Taylor, Sean, Adam, and Vincent*

Acknowledgments

There are many people to whom I am grateful for their influence on my life or this collection directly. I cannot name them all, but I will start with Professor Nelson Bentley for encouraging me as a 52 year old student to stay enrolled in his English 101 class at the University of Washington. Without his urging I would have dropped the course.

I will be forever grateful to Frances McCue, Founding Director of the Hugo House, and a dear friend who opened for me the world of poetry. I remember walking into the Hugo House, and her warm welcome making me comfortable and subsequently a regular at Hugo House events. I had an opportunity to work with very caring instructors who inspired me to continue to write prose and poetry.

I would like to thank my children Roberta, Martin, and Teresa for encouraging me to put my writing into a book, and my son Victor who helped put it together. I hope my children can feel through my poetry the life in the internment camps I never shared with them when they were growing up.

I would like to thank my Issei parents who inspired me through their endurance and perseverance. And I would like to thank my grandchildren for making my life full and at age 88, still desiring to learn, so that I can tell them my stories and leave with them a legacy of the cultural values of my parents.

~Suma Yagi

Contents

P   i
   A Japanese Name   1

S   I. T   E   Y
   Two-Syllable Words   7
   Yutampo   8
   Years Apart   10
     e First Day   12

S   II. M   P
   If Hills Had Voices …   17
   Mama's Voyage to America   19
   Mama's Notebook   20
   Mama's Citizenship   21
   Papa's Way   22
   Papa's Canvas Bag   23

S   III. D   ,
   Another Day of Infamy   29
   December 1941   30

S   IV. C   H
   Camp Harmony Assembly Center   37
   Mess Hall   40
   In the Barracks   41
     e Day After   42
     e Unfolding   44
   Solitude   45

S   V. M

A Dark Cloud Hovered over …   51
From One Prison to Another   53
    e View   55
Arriving at Minidoka   56
Papa Block 16 – Mess Hall Cook   58
America Your Country   60

S   VI.   MIS

Nisei Soldier Dreaming   65
Go for Broke   66
    e Same Uniform   68
America's Secret Weapon   69
American Heroes   70
Haruo Returns   72

S   VII. L   B

Wounds Still Open   77
Citizenship behind the Steel Door   88
Tribute to Our Issei   91
    e Legacy of Lights Out   93
    I   ank Aki   95
    e First Poems   97

N   101
P   C   117
A   A   119
A   E   119

Preface

In 1942, I was a displaced teenager, pulled away from my home and placed in an internment camp under Executive Order 9066. I realize now how important it is to share personal experiences as part of my Nisei heritage. Just as important to the Issei legacy are the words *gaman* (patience, perseverance), *ōn* (obligation, gratitude) *haji* (shame, dishonor), and *shikkari* (endure, bear up), words used freely by my Issei parents and personified in their lives, leaving indelible imprints and shaping our Nisei souls.

Not only were we Niseis beneficiaries of strong family values, but we also inherited the essence of community through churches, kenjinkais (people who came from a certain prefecture in Japan), judo, and kendo tournaments, and Japanese school picnics supported by the Isseis. We also witnessed strong bonds of friendships. I remember as a young woman being startled when my mother talked about her friendships of seventy years. "Seventy years! at seems incredible," I often said. Now I too am experiencing friendships that began with my Baptist church nursery playmates seventy years ago.

My Nisei disposition sometimes makes me uncomfortable when sharing personal experiences about my cultural heritage, and yet I feel a special responsibility to both past and future generations. It is important that we allow the Sanseis and future generations to hear our voices. My voice is but a small part of the choir of Niseis but carries similar rhythms, harmonies, and discords. It is equally important that we let these voices resonate beyond our own community to erase misconceptions and stimulate education, understanding, and tolerance. I want to give a voice to people whose voices have not been heard.

It is when we bring pen to paper and record our experiences that we allow others to share the emotions of past events. Today I am hearing voices of Sanseis saying, "You Niseis must tell your story for us." For the most part, we Niseis find it di cult to expose our souls.

We select a limited audience, and only when it is required do we share our stories, our images of a wounding past.

Twenty five years ago, while writing about childhood memories for a writing class assignment, I was surprised to discover emotions of pain and disillusionment surfacing. Only recently have I allowed myself to resurrect those feelings, to let emotions form, and to let the tears flow freely.

Issei – Japanese immigrant to the U.S. - first generation

Nisei – U.S. born child of Japanese immigrant – second generation

Sansei – U.S. born grandchild of Japanese immigrant – third generation

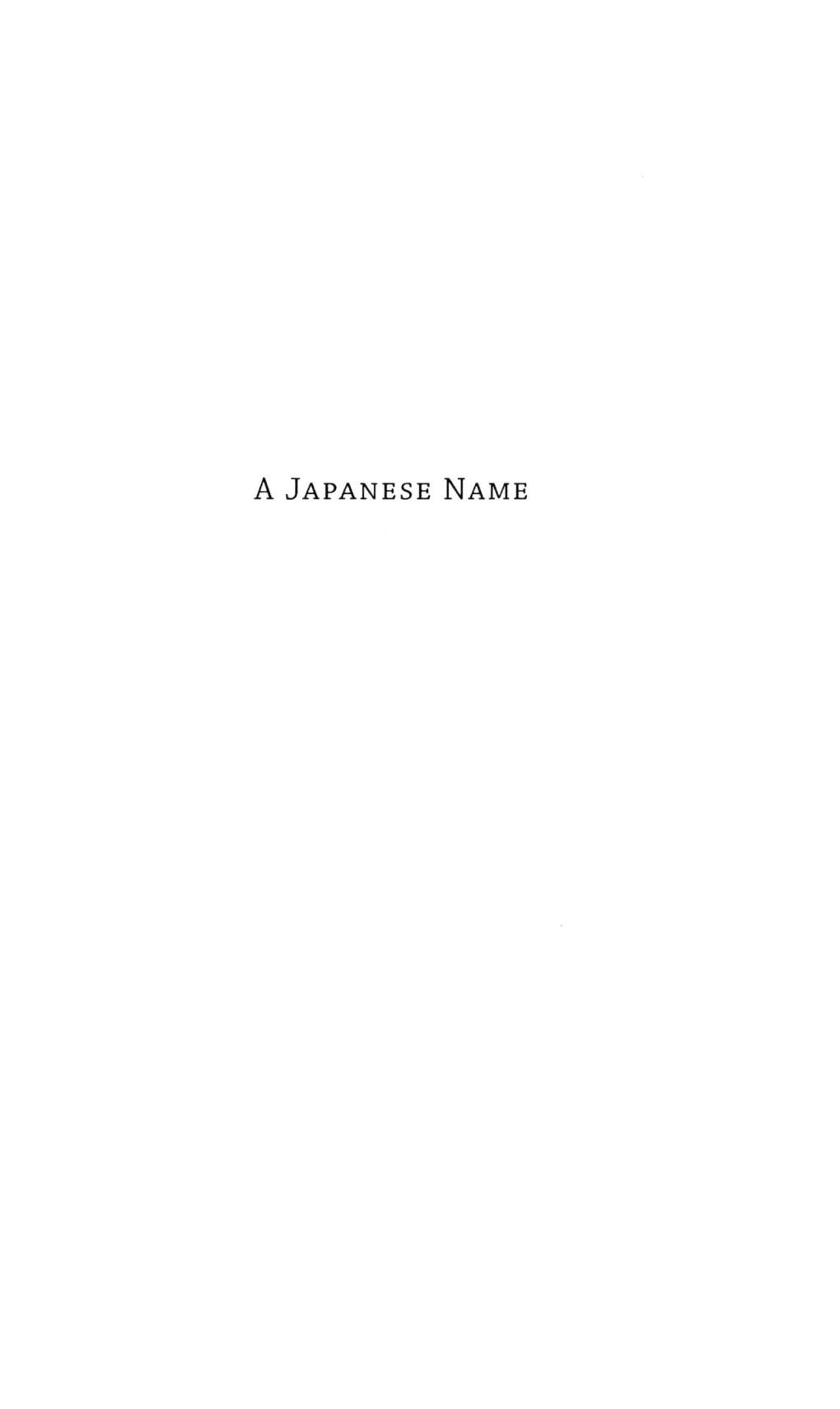

A Japanese Name

A Japanese Name

My daughter was ten then:
"Mommy, why didn't you name me Shigeko or Midori
or some other Japanese name?"

"Roberta Lynn is such a pretty name.
We chose it especially for you."
My heart smothered words too tearful to speak.

When I was her age,
at the start of each school day,
students would gather to salute the flag.

At first my baby finger would slip from under my thumb,
while I brought the other three fingers to my eyebrow.
Soon my hand curved with ease.

The word *indivisible* stymied my tongue,
but the pledge soon flowed like gentle water.
"My country 'tis of thee, sweet land of liberty
of thee I sing" soothed my vocal cords each day.

We children enacted historical events at school assemblies:
I was a Pilgrim, drowning in yards of black muslin,
set off by a white, full-body apron and a lady's bonnet.
Mama sewed them by hand.

I knelt on the shore of Massachusetts.
I thanked God for the plentiful harvest.
I was at the signing of the Declaration of Independence,
where our brown, yellow, and white hands moved across the parchment.

The Thomas Jeffersons with different voices intoned:
"All men are created equal. They are endowed with certain unalienable rights.
Among these are life, liberty, and the pursuit of happiness."

Every pore opened to these promises;
the fiber of my being responded.
We children—Asian, African, European—
were bubbles in the melting pot.
They needed me.

December 7, 1941: Japan Bombs Pearl Harbor

I responded, "Isn't it horrible that Japan bombed our country and attacked us?"

Our voices of allegiance were muted.
The US government severed ties to
progenies with Japanese names.

Two weeks following all this
an eight o'clock curfew restricted me to my home,
while others remained outside.
Some children withdrew handshakes.

Signs on telephone poles publicly announced our indictment:
Executive Order 9066, tacked by nails, ordered our mass evacuation.

Treasures I'd gathered during my fourteen years
could not be squeezed into the two suitcases allotted each person.
My heart remained in the stuffed bear,
in the box of my favorite valentine cards,
with my Shirley Temple doll,
abandoned to find their way
to some other child's home.

I was interned in a camp with the rest of my family,
a place where rattlesnakes and coyotes made permanent homes.

The six of us squeezed into an eighteen-by-twenty-foot room.
Barbed wire enclosed our new quarters,
guarded by soldiers with guns in watchtowers.

When my child asked why I didn't give her a Japanese name,
I could only respond:
"Roberta Lynn is such a pretty name.
We chose it especially for you."

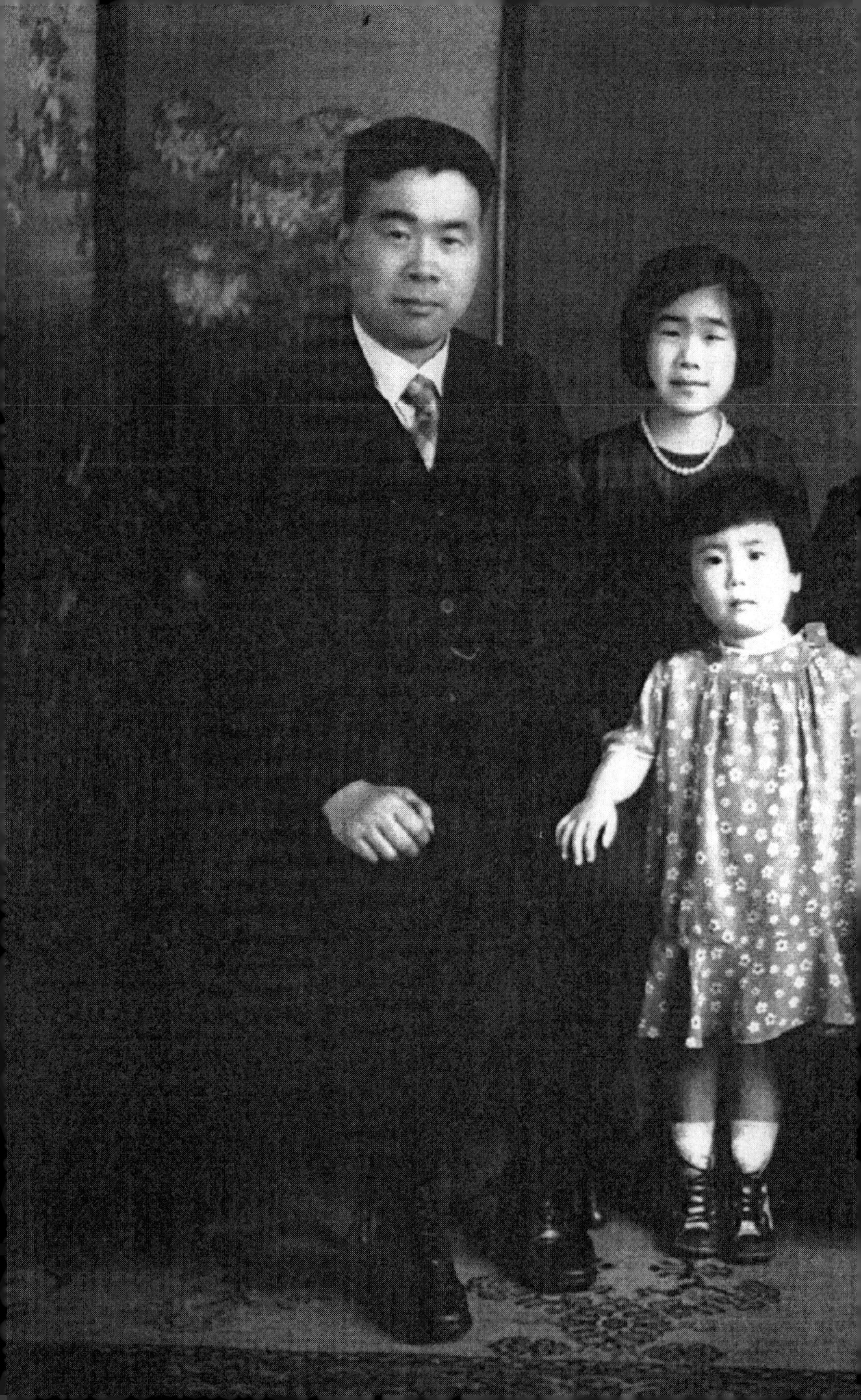

SECTION I.

The Early Years

Overleaf: The Kato Family Front Row: Suma and Aki
Back Row, Haruotoshi, Fusae, Murako, Haruo, and family friend

Two-Syllable Words

Dedicated to my mother, Murako Okamura Kato, who nurtured me with these words.

Every evening we would gather around the large round table.
With our meals, Mama would serve two-syllable words.
Between bites of food, Mama would say:

"Remember *gaman* and *enryo*.
Do not bring *haji* to the family.
Remember *giri* to the family.
Remember *on* to the family."

We children could feel the load of our family on our small backs.
We could never quite understand why two-syllable words felt so heavy.

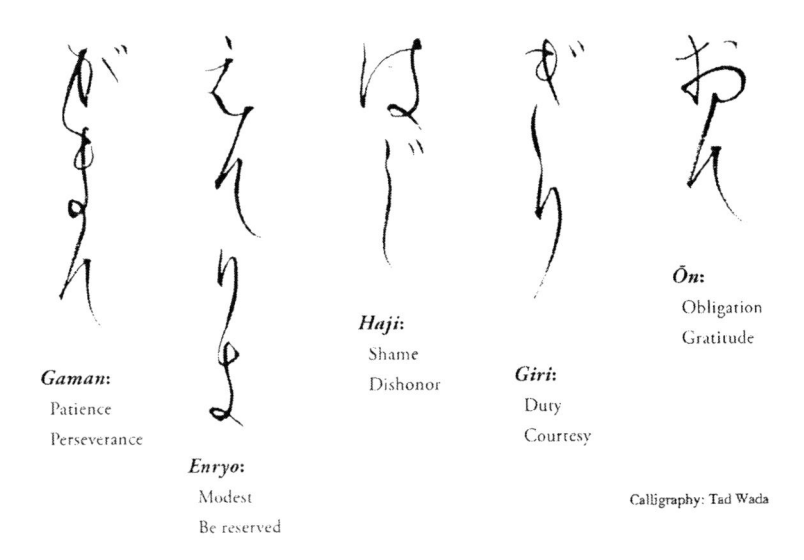

Gaman:
Patience
Perseverance

Enryo:
Modest
Be reserved

Haji:
Shame
Dishonor

Giri:
Duty
Courtesy

Ōn:
Obligation
Gratitude

Calligraphy: Tad Wada

Yutampos

During the cold winter nights,
my two sisters and I stood around the large coal stove,
waiting for Mama to put hot water, steaming from the kettle,
into the yutampos.

Mama made sure we took turns between the bright aluminum, oval-shaped one
and the rectangular one of heavy rubber.
We were glad when we got the aluminum one,
since the rubber yutampo had a musty odor.

Mama sewed bags of colorful, heavy flannel cloth.
She carefully put the yutampos in them
so we wouldn't burn ourselves.
We carried them by the long drawstrings.
Sometimes, Mama would give us a sugar cookie.

Mama shooed us through the swinging door between the kitchen and bedroom
into the cold bedroom, warning us to be careful.

We would position the yutampos beneath the sheets
before climbing into our bed.
We would slide our feet until we found the warm spot.

Gradually, the yutampos ended up in our arms,
as we held them like children hugging stuffed animals.
They warmed us during the cold winter nights.

By morning, they no longer provided warmth.
We would find them on the floor next to our beds.

Years Apart

The Yesler Housing Project consumes the entire hill—
not a hint of the old neighborhood.

Most of the houses standing one next to the other
have shingles that slap like hands in the wind,
and the paint on the houses looks like scaly skin.

Our house is the most elegant on the block.
It has the longest wooden stairways;
each stair creaks a different tone.

Blades of grass creep between the cracks.
They tickle my leg or slip between my toes
when I take off my shoes.

The monstrous stove dominates our small kitchen.
Papa struggles to roll the big wooden barrel into the room.
He fills it halfway with water from a hose connected outside.

Mama follows right behind.
She pours boiling hot water from the tea kettle humming on the stove.

My sister and I jump into the makeshift bathtub.
"Sato-imo! Sato-imo!"
Mama would say, scrubbing us together.

Satoimo –Taro root or "Japanese potato"

Light from the overhead bulb casts shadows on the bottom of the barrel.

My sister and I make believe we've fallen into a deep, dark well.

We splash our hands, then walk our fingers up the wall inside the barrel.

Mama never punishes us for spilling water.

We love to watch.

Water creeps like little streams,

following the slant of the floor toward the back door.

Our kitchen is so unique,

even the floor slants a special way.

The First Day

Mama kept saying:
"*Haree* (hurry), *haree*, Suma.
You going to be late."

I looked down at my black patent shoes,
glistening like tap dancer's shoes.
My feet had flirted with them all week long.

The day had arrived.
Mama said I could wear them on the first day of school.

The sidewalk seemed to grab my shoes.
Each step felt heavy.

I reached out.
I held Mama's hand like a starfish
holds on to its prey.

My tongue like a windshield wiper
wiped the tears that trickled near the
edge of my mouth.
It salted the mush in my stomach.

"I don't feel good. I want to go home."
"Mama," I said.
"I don't feel good. I want to go home."

I put my hands in the dark corner of my pockets.
They enjoyed the momentary refuge.

I placed my feet firmly on the sidewalk
that was pulling at my feet.

Mama pulled my arms.
She put her hands over my clenched fist
like candy wrapping.

I felt determination in her hands as she
pulled me.

Mama met some of her friends with their children.
Their children wore different shoes.
The sidewalk did not grab them.
Their steps were buoyant.

Mama started bowing like a pigeon that was picking up
food on the sidewalk.
She hid her face between bows.

Mama said in Japanese,
"My other children never acted this way.
She is the baby of the family.
She is very spoiled."

Section II.
Mama and Papa

*Overleaf: Haruotoshi and Murako Kato, Suma's father and mother.
Photo taken on the lawn in front of the Eleanor Apartments building they owned*

If hills had voices, First Hill on Twelfth Avenue and Main Street in Seattle would have bellowed, "Here we are alive! These are happy times."

In 1934, a single-story frame house sat on the south side at the foot of the hill. The Yoshida family lived on the main floor, while the Japanese Congregational Church met in the basement. Next door was a row house, one part living quarters for the Ishii family, and the other part a Japanese language school named Ishii Gakko (Mr. Ishii's School).

Built next to the school were single homes shared by two or three families of Japanese immigrants with their American-born children: the Hirata, Kawase, Shigihara, and Kusakabe families. At the end of the hill, an empty lot overgrown with tall weeds and covered with debris could be found after a large drop.

The driveway to a Texaco gas station and four two-story houses were on the north side of First Hill. It seemed that all of the two-story single-family dwellings had more than one family living in them, which accounted for the large number of children in those few homes. The first was shared by the Kato, Amabe, and Yamashita families. Next to it was the house in which the Taniguchi, Aoyama, and Suzuki families lived. Behind that was where the Ichikawa family resided.

The thirty-five Nisei children formed strong bonds, sharing the unpaved, rocky hill as their playground. They formed teams among themselves, using telephone posts on each side of the hill as bases for their game of *gintori*. It was common to see children as young as six or seven joining their teenage siblings and running helter-skelter up and down the hill. Boys collected milk tops and played among themselves; girls played with beanbags filled with red beans, sacks sewn by their mothers.

The Japanese Buddhist Church, located at the crest of the hill, was the only church actually built as a church and not converted from a residence. It seemed almost boastful in contrast to the others. It had a stairwell on both sides leading up to a large covered porch. Big doors opened to an entryway where the aroma of incense hung in the air. The gold-laced archway in front of the altar where a large Buddha sat gave it an aura of elegance and urged reverence.

I wished my family attended that church instead of the Japanese Congregational Church, where we worshiped in tiny quarters; sat on hard, wooden folding chairs; and felt the dankness of the basement penetrate our bodies. The children who attended the Buddhist church always had a *senbe* (Japanese cookie) in their hands as they left it, much to the envy of the children who attended the Japanese Congregational Church.

Ironically, a few yards away from the church, the hill curved into a red-light district, where cobblestone streets and sidewalks started and the dirt road of our hill ended. As children, we never quite understood why those ladies (as we heard people refer to them) tapped, tapped, tapped at the windows as men walked by.

Mama's Voyage to America

Answering her father's letter,
Mama boarded the *Hikawa Maru*.
A future husband in America awaited her.

The many moods of the ocean water
became her moods. A calm, serene
ocean—not a ripple, a sheet of glass—

turned into a playful sea. Waves rolled
and danced, then turned turbulent,
rearing crests of four to five feet,

pushing the boat from side to side.
Her stomach cushioned each movement.
She held on to the deck railings while

heaving what she had eaten, leaving a
trail in the sea. She longed for her
mother back in Japan.

As the boat slowed down by the dock,
she noticed a man resembling the photo
of her father. He was looking up at her.

Mama's Notebook

Mama's eyes twinkle with pride
as she turns the pages of her notebook
for her children to see.

The Constitution's words,
formed by lines, twisting, swirling like ballerinas holding hands,
Spread across the page.

Japanese characters—
straight, sticklike figures (*kata kana*)—
sit on top of each vowel in cursive.

Mama would say the *kata kana* helps her
remember how the instructor sounds out the word.
Mama moves her lips,
shaping each word before her mouth lets go.

Each syllable carries her determination
as she recites the Bill of Rights aloud
for her children's ears.

Mama would then ask us
You know this?
Then how about this?

Mama's eyes light up.
She is pleased she knows the Amendments
Better than her children do.

Mama's Citizenship, September 1953

Mama came home,
her voice dancing on sound waves,
her eyes glowing
as she told us that she
stood all by herself before the federal judge,
taking the oath of allegiance
as an American citizen.

Until her death at ninety-three,
Mama wore her citizenship like a badge of honor.

Mama would say, "I vote every time, and
my voting record at my precinct would show it."
Just as the sun rises each morning,
each Election Day,
I could expect a phone call from Mama.
"Mama, it's only 7:45.
I'm just drinking my coffee and reading the papers."

A high-pitched, excited voice on the other end of the line:
"Did you vote? I already vote. Good-bye."

Papa's Way

He reminded me of Buddha:
his pear-shaped head completely bald,
silvery threads trimming his temples,
his almond-shaped eyes lost in the fullness of his face,
his shoulders too small for his wide round waist.

Like so many immigrants, Papa was beckoned
by the lady carrying a torch off the shores of New York.
She did not face the Pacific, but her promise
of the American Dream called all the way to Japan.

Papa worked over a hot stove. All of the chairs inside
the small café were filled with men with unkempt hair;
their bodies smelled of urine and sweat.
They worked along the waterfront and had huge appetites.
Mama carried heavy plates of food.

One day Papa put a sign on the door:
"CLOSED—OUT OF BUSINESS."

Papa's Canvas Bag

Papa discarded his cook's hat—frayed at the seams—
the one that had covered his head like a deflated balloon.
Instead, he donned a Red Cap that fit snugly
as he carried baggage for train passengers
at the King Street Station. Passengers would put into Papa's

hands loose change, which he would slip into his pocket,
the coins clicking against each other with the movement
of his body. Soon Papa was answering to the nickname
"Happy." Each night, by the large kitchen table, Papa
would pull his pockets inside out and empty them.

The beige muslin cloth hung from both sides
of his waist like droopy donkey ears. Papa would finger
the nickels, dimes, quarters in separate piles, dreaming
of warm food piled on dinner plates, thick overcoats,
new shoes, and school supplies for his four children.

Papa would cup his left hand around the coin wrapper.
With his right hand, he would pinch the coins between
his thumb and forefingers and drop them into the tube,
folding down the edges until the ends lapped over
like origami, sealing the coins inside.

Papa would then bring out a tablet, edges of the pages
curled by time and by his fingers. He'd record amounts
in three columns, return the tablet to a box in his
bedroom, and then place the wrapped coins into
a green canvas bag. He carried it to the bank.

One day Papa called all of us together around the
kitchen table. His voice sang, "We move. We go see."
Several days later, we all squeezed into a car
driven by Papa's friend. As we turned from Eighteenth and Yesler,
our eyes became half moons, corners of lips turned upward.

Oohs! and *Ahhs!* poured out of our mouths.
The apartment had wide concrete stairs.
Rubber balls bounced like grasshoppers off the steps.
The wooden stairs at our old house hid them
under the planks, trapped in the grass.

I thought of the wooden barrel in our old house.
Each night, Papa rolled it, four feet high,
from outside the door into the kitchen.
Mama poured water from a large tea kettle sitting on a coal stove.
My sister and I would wrap our arms around our knees,

pretending we were in a deserted well, inhaling the stale
smell of the water-soaked wood. Rays from the overhead
light did not reach the bottom. We washed the dirt from
our bodies and walked our fingers up the barrel's wall,
while our mother scrubbed us like *sataimo*, potatoes.

I still feel the warmth of my first bath at our new home:
two light fixtures, fancy frosted glass and scalloped hems
placed on each side of the mirror, brought light with a click.

The bathtub was white as snow, smooth and shiny;
the end of the tub slanted upward at an angle.

I could rest my head, keeping it above the water,
even while stretching. I could even wiggle my toes,
pushing little waves of warm water over me.
I felt like a princess as I inhaled the fragrance of
lavender soap, and closed my eyes.

One day Papa brought home a box of chalk. We used
the sticks to draw hopscotch rectangles on the sidewalk,
joining the other children. Mama cut squares
from bright cotton and filled them with *azuki*, red beans.
Then she sewed up the sides. We would jump—

spreading our feet apart, making sure both feet
landed within each square. Balancing on one foot,
we tossed the beanbags inside the lines while Papa
made us laugh until we lost our balance.
You could hear our screeching: "*Papa! Papa!*"

As Papa turned, we could see his eyes almost
disappear; the muscles of his face pushed his
fat cheeks toward his temples, and his mouth
widened into a smile.

WESTERN DEFENSE COMMAND AND FOURTH ARMY
WARTIME CIVIL CONTROL ADMINISTRATION
Presidio of San Francisco, California
April 24, 1942

INSTRUCTIONS TO ALL PERSONS OF JAPANESE ANCESTRY

Living in the Following Area:

All that portion of the City of Seattle, State of Washington, lying generally south of an east-west line beginning at the point at which Jackson Street meets Elliott Bay; thence easterly along Jackson Street to Fifth Avenue; thence southerly on Fifth Avenue to Dearborn Street; thence easterly on Dearborn Street to Twenty-third Avenue; thence northerly on Twenty-third Avenue to Yesler Way; thence easterly on Yesler Way to Lake Washington.

Pursuant to the provisions of Civilian Exclusion Order No. 18, this Headquarters, dated April 24, 1942, all persons of Japanese ancestry, both alien and non-alien, will be evacuated from the above area by 12 o'clock noon, P. W. T., Friday, May 1, 1942.

No Japanese person living in the above area will be permitted to change residence after 12 o'clock noon, P. W. T., Friday, April 24, 1942, without obtaining special permission from the representative of the Commanding General, Northwestern Sector, at the Civil Control Station located at:

1319 Rainier Avenue, Seattle, Washington.

Such permits will only be granted for the purpose of uniting members of a family, or in cases of grave emergency.

The Civil Control Station is equipped to assist the Japanese population affected by this evacuation in the following ways:

1. Give advice and instructions on the evacuation.
2. Provide services with respect to the management, leasing, sale, storage or other disposition of most kinds of property, such as real estate, business and professional equipment, household goods, boats, automobiles and livestock.
3. Provide temporary residence elsewhere for all Japanese in family groups.
4. Transport persons and a limited amount of clothing and equipment to their new residence.

The Following Instructions Must Be Observed:

1. A responsible member of each family, preferably the head of the family, or the person in whose name most of the property is held, and each individual living alone, will report to the Civil Control Station to receive further instructions. This must be done between 8:00 A. M. and 5:00 P. M. on Saturday, April 25, 1942, or between 8:00 A. M. and 5:00 P. M. on Sunday, April 26, 1942.

2. Evacuees must carry with them on departure for the Assembly Center, the following property:
   (a) Bedding and linens (no mattress) for each member of the family;
   (b) Toilet articles for each member of the family;
   (c) Extra clothing for each member of the family;
   (d) Sufficient knives, forks, spoons, plates, bowls and cups for each member of the family;
   (e) Essential personal effects for each member of the family.

All items carried will be securely packaged, tied and plainly marked with the name of the owner and numbered in accordance with instructions obtained at the Civil Control Station.

The size and number of packages is limited to that which can be carried by the individual or family group.

3. No pets of any kind will be permitted.

4. The United States Government through its agencies will provide for the storage at the sole risk of the owner of the more substantial household items, such as iceboxes, washing machines, pianos and other heavy furniture. Cooking utensils and other small items will be accepted for storage if crated, packed and plainly marked with the name and address of the owner. Only one name and address will be used by a given family.

5. Each family, and individual living alone, will be furnished transportation to the Assembly Center or will be authorized to travel by private automobile in a supervised group. All instructions pertaining to the movement will be obtained at the Civil Control Station.

Go to the Civil Control Station between the hours of 8:00 A. M. and 5:00 P. M., Saturday, April 25, 1942, or between the hours of 8:00 A. M. and 5:00 P. M., Sunday, April 26, 1942, to receive further instructions.

J. L. DeWITT
Lieutenant General, U. S. Army
Commanding

SEE CIVILIAN EXCLUSION ORDER NO. 18.

Section III.

December 7th, 1941

Overleaf left: Instructions posted in Seattle instructing Japanese Americans how to comply with the evacuation decree.
Photo courtesy of Densho: The Japanese American Legacy Project

Overleaf right: Soldier nailing placards containing Civilian Exclusion Order No. 1 and special instructions to all Japanese residents of Bainbridge Island.
Photo courtesy of the Museum of History & Industry

Another Day of Infamy

The fireballs engulfing Pearl Harbor
reverberated a day of infamy
across the Pacific to the shores of the United States.

The United States government disowned progenies
With almond-shaped eyes and Japanese names.

By the stroke of the pen,
The United States government issued Executive Order 9066,
deposing "inalienable rights and due process,"
designating the Northwest and California
as Military Areas One, Two, and Three.

The Constitution was bent:
Those in power
failed to acknowledge the American soul
of Japanese Americans.
They saw them through the clouded lens of racism,
their loyalty questionable—potential saboteurs.
They used "military necessity" for their removal.

The Constitution was bent:
Those in power listened to the voices
of those who would gain
thousands of acres of lands
made fertile and bountiful
by the hard, weather-beaten hands,
by the long hours and strong backs
of Japanese American farmers.

December 1941

Our lives turned like a glass jar
flipped upside down, suffocating us.
Hairline cracks grew deep and wide
until the glass shattered and our world
collapsed.

Our citizenship buried
in the folds of our eyelids, we were
spoofed in cartoons—our eyes were
slanted under horn-rimmed glasses,
our teeth protruding like the mouths
of beavers—kinsfolk of Tojo and Hirohito.

We felt the jab of words: "sneaky,"
"unworthy," "treacherous," "disloyal."
"Herd 'em up, pack 'em off,"
"Put 'em inside badlands" appeared
in newsprint and over sound waves.
We discovered these were not words for the enemy,
but for anyone of Japanese ancestry.
We citizens were no longer
wrapped in the arms of our country.

In the play-yard at school, my classmate's
hand withdrew from mine, reaching instead
to someone else, leaving a gap in the line
where our hands once linked together.

Another girl cupped her hand
around a classmate's ear.
"She's a Jap," I could hear.

Soon we were installed inside
another jar, one not sheathed in glass,
but the walls of our home.
Shortly after the bombing, we were
shut away each night, held under curfew.
We felt the hands of the clocks
wrapping around us like a python.

No more basketball games.
No more school activities.
No more cheering the teams.
No more judo lessons.
No more scout meetings.
After dinner no more
walks to the library where I'd join
my brother and sisters and friends,
their voices and laughter filling the air.

Signs started to appear on telephone posts
and walls throughout the city.
In each nail, we felt man's inhumanity
toward man, pinching into the wood.

The government allowed us eight days
to dismantle our lives into crates
that we'd abandon or store. People we'd
never met appeared at our doorstep.
They left with boxes.
A man gave my brother twenty dollars,
then drove away with his car.

Mama wore her heavy coat,
collar trimmed with fur and
her hat with flowers along the brim.
Papa wore his best suit and fedora.
We needed to wear as much as we could.
We children layered our woolens.

We squeezed what we could in the suitcases
until threads frayed; some clothing stuck out.
We pushed utensils into the boxes.
Forks and knives poked through.

No room for photos. Gone were
Mama's and Papa's families back in Japan.
No room for my stuffed animals.
Good-bye to the new Shirley Temple doll,
to my Good Citizenship Certificate.

Tags around our necks, we boarded
the buses. Our names became
family number 117007.

The bus driver took us through the city streets
onto the highway. He kept his eyes to the horizon
and did not speak. The motor strained
and I thought of the dogs we'd all left behind,
their barks fainter and fainter.
Tears salted my mouth.

Across fields where I spent summers
picking strawberries, where the Isseis once
bent in the hot sun, the bus slowed. We came to
the Puyallup Fairgrounds, where every fall
I came to the fair, scenes floating inside me,
then popping like popcorn.

Now it was Camp Harmony Assembly Center,
a name given by the government for an
American concentration camp, where the
fair used to be—a place we once loved.
Last fall, I'd run the rides until the tickets were gone.
I was happy knowing I would be
returning the following year.

Against the background of the merry-go-round
and Ferris wheels, we came off the bus and
climbed down each step. Soldiers holding rifles
followed us with their guns. Their eyes never left us.

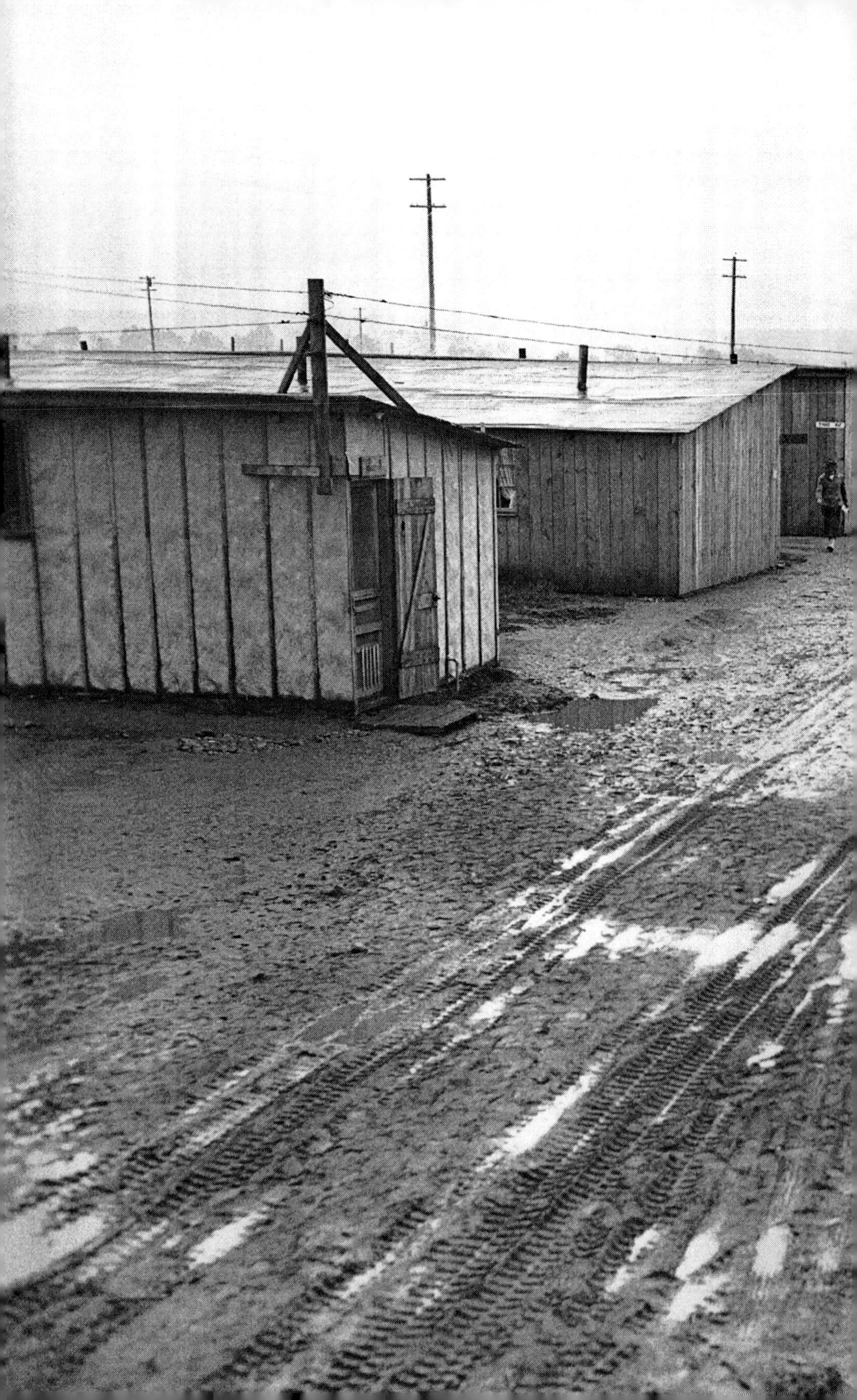

Section IV.

Camp Harmony

Overleaf: Muddy conditions around the barracks at the Puyallup Assembly Center, also known as "Camp Harmony." It was constructed on the racetrack of the Puyallup fairgrounds. The Assembly Center was open from April 28 - September 23, 1942
Photo courtesy of the Museum of History & Industry, Seattle Post-Intelligencer Collection

Camp Harmony Assembly Center

(*The name given by the government to the temporary encampment built on the Puyallup Fairgrounds*)

In seventeen days
"Five million board feet of lumber
For a city of 8000 Japs."

The parking lot of the Puyallup Fairgrounds
was suddenly turned upside down
to squeaking sounds of steam shovels,
the banging and clanging of hammers.

Forty rows of boxlike buildings,
covered with tar paper,
became areas A, B, and C of Camp Harmony.
Two-by-fours were laid on the ground,
planks nailed for floors,
slits left for blades of grass and worms.

The fairgrounds became Area D, Camp Harmony.
Barracks were built in the heart of race tracks.
Horse stalls were converted into living quarters;
internees replaced animals.

Odor of manure hung on walls like wallpaper.
Internees carried the heavy stench on their skin.
As the days grew warmer, the odor became stronger,
leaving permanent imprints.

An internee remarked after almost a lifetime,
"I still can't forget the stench of the manure."

Six rooms—eight by ten—
were separated by a wallboard that did not reach the ceiling.
Privacy was lost as the cries of babies, coughs,
snoring, sneezes, whispers, and lovemaking
became vibrations on sound waves
moving through the three feet of open space.

Barbed wires like corkscrews
twisted around the perimeter of the camp,
lacing the top of a nine-foot fence.

Internees were given canvas bags and pitchforks
to stuff straw piled at end of the barrack.

They wrestled the straw into the canvas bags,
combing the unruly straws with a pitchfork.
The straws scratched back and drew red lines on their skin.

They shoved the swollen bags on top of cots.
Sticks of straw poked through.

Internees walked a distance of a city block
to community mess halls,
where they lined up for meals
three times each day.

Children soon sought other children to sit with;
parents were left with other parents.

Families became broken fragments
of Executive Order 9066.

Mess Hall

Internees listened for a voice bellowing on a bullhorn
from the mess hall where hundreds crowded together
for every meal—breakfast, lunch, and dinner.

They walked a distance of a city block and a half
on roads bulldozers sprinkled broken pieces of rock,
clumps of dirt and left holes where rain water settled

It was especially difficult for the elderly to walk.
Shoes felt heavy from dirt sticking to the soles.
And in their hands, they held a plate, a cup, and utensils.

The elderly with canes needed assistance of family members.
Young children were restless; they wanted something to eat,
puzzled why their parents would not give them food.

They stood outside next to the building, no protection
from the rain and hot sun; they inched their way inside,
then waited again in long lines inside the mess hall.
Their first meal—Vienna sausage, a potato, a slice of bread.

In the Barracks

There was no running water in our one-room quarters.
We took our toothbrushes and towels out of our suitcases, and
we rushed to the community bathroom, only to discover
people were squeezed on both sides of the rectangular
galvanized sink, leaving no room for my sister and me.

We kept our eyes pinned to the line, moving rapidly
to the spot a person appeared to be leaving, then sliding
into the space they left behind. I squeezed my arms tightly
against my body as I moved my toothbrush in short
up-and-down strokes, not like my usual way of swinging

my arms like a ballerina, dancing over and around my molars.
I saw my spit mix with other peoples's saliva as the water
turned it into a bubbling mixture and sent it down the drain.
My stomach felt queasy. My sister and I ran back to our
room as April showers poured down on us.
The rain joined the tears that trickled down my cheeks.

As we walked into our one-room home, we discovered
there was no place we could hang our wet clothes, not one
hook on the wall, no shelf, no table, no chairs. We draped
them over our suitcases, the ones that held the only possessions
we were allowed to bring under Executive Order 9066.

Shortly after we returned, we heard a knock on the door.
A soldier with a clipboard was checking to make sure we were
complying with the 9:30 p.m. curfew. As he left, he barked,
"It's lights out at 10:30." He looked at us with piercing eyes.

The Day After

All night, the straw poked through.
I had to wait for daylight.
Shiplap partitions separating the rooms
reached partway to the ceiling.
Snoring and conversation commingled—
cries of babies, coughs, sneezes, laughter.

We felt our way through the dark
to the community latrine,
more than a block away.
We scraped our feet to find
our way in the darkness.

The outhouse holes, six on each side,
formed a large domino across the room.
Rows of buttocks to the right, to the left,
buttocks abutting buttocks, we tried to find our place.

Then an *aka-tunk* sound: water
gushed through the galvanized sheeting,
spraying buttocks and taking with it
anything in its path.

At the community shower, a block and a half
from the outhouse, we lined up like cattle
in front of a trough. Our bodies naked,
we stood face-to-face. Water squeezed from
holes in a one-inch pipe that ran along the room.

A few days later, during our meal,
my sister whispered, "Let's go and take a shower now."
We gulped our food while others ate.

We stood under the pipes,
next to each other,
letting water flow onto our naked bodies
without others in front of us.
Then, we noticed,
other young girls started to join us.

The Unfolding

Behind the barbed wires of Camp Harmony,
Mama and Papa unwrapped meanings of words.
Shikkari (keeping one's head high in the face of adversity).
Gaman (accepting and enduring without complaint).

As we were growing up, how often we heard
Mama say these words. Here, we tested our words.
Mama and Papa added a new expression:
Shikata ga nai (it cannot be helped).

Solitude

I miss you.
With you I shared so much.
My thoughts were naked
and unclothed.

You were always
behind the bedroom door,
but here there are no private doors.
My cot, US government issue,
crowds next to five others:
my father, mother, brother, and two sisters.

Each night I hear every movement,
every breath,
as they sleep beside me.

The bathrooms are no different:
a community latrine,
two boards with outhouse holes
in rows like dots on dominoes.
We turn our buttocks toward each other
and squat.
Camp plumbing flushes through.

Showers are no different.
We shower in rows.
A pipe with tiny holes
sprays us like cattle
at a trough.

Perhaps it is well you are a stranger.
Thoughts allowed to be naked
would hurt too much.

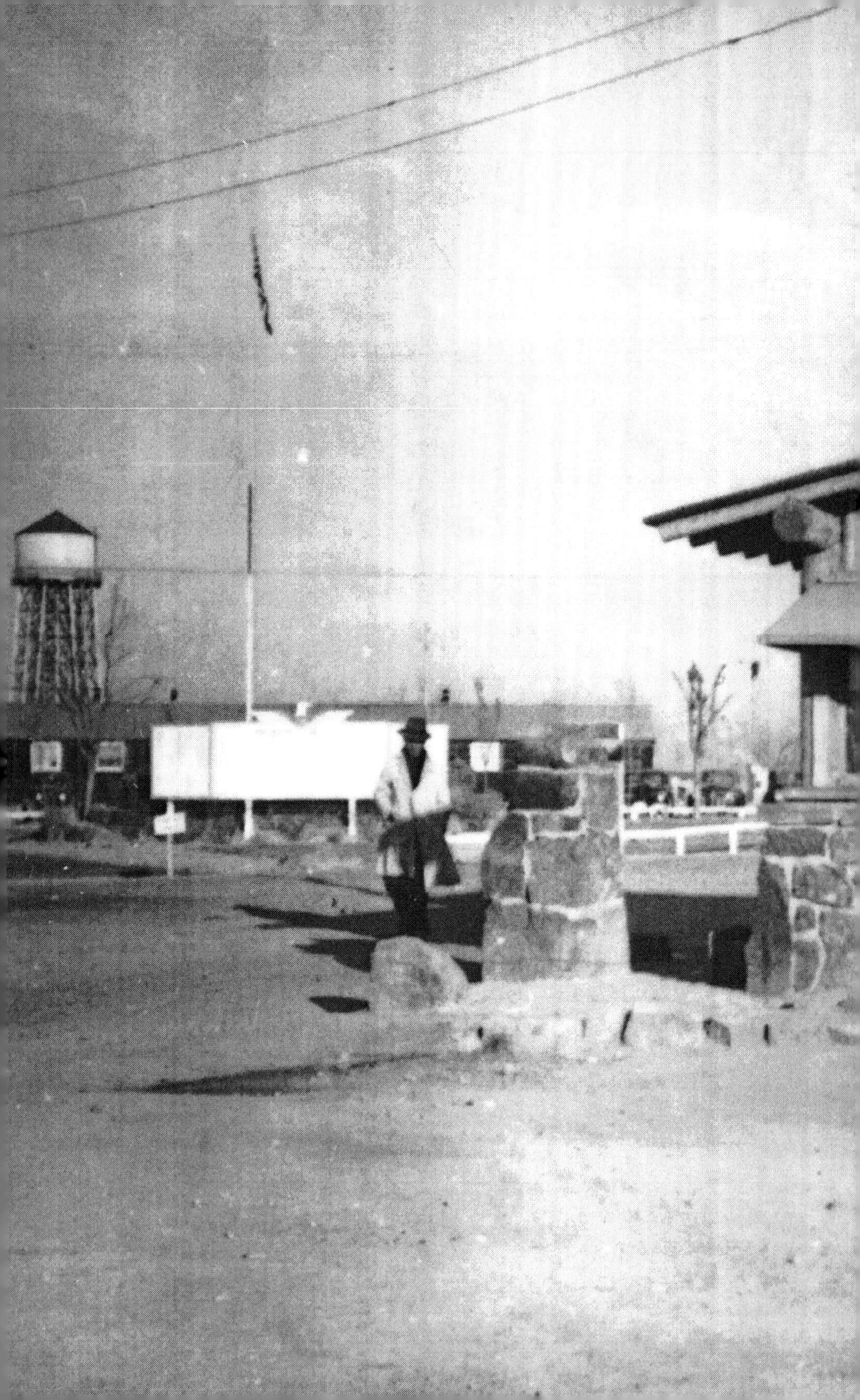

Section V.

Minidoka

Overleaf: Man and woman in front of the camp guard house at the Minidoka concentration camp, aka, "Relocation Center."
Photo courtesy of the Wing Luke Museum, the Hatate Collection

A dark cloud hovered over Camp Harmony. There was word that "evacuees" would be transferred to a "semipermanent" internment camp. Then, four months after we had arrived at the camp, came the cloudburst. Our friends and families started being transferred to the Minidoka Concentration Camp. The concentration camp encompassed thirty-three thousand acres, six hundred buildings, five miles of barbed-wire fencing, and eight guard towers on a barren desert.

Eager to move internees into the camp within the interior of the United States, the US government started relocating five hundred people per day. Harry Stafford, appointed as director of the center, wired the Western Defense Command to gain permission for those remaining in Camp Harmony Assembly Center to be kept there for ten days so that construction work at Minidoka Concentration Camp could be completed. His plea was ignored.

On August 20, 1942, those of us confined in Area B were escorted by armed soldiers to a large area of the fairgrounds where a fleet of buses awaited. Evacuees confined to Area D had already been sent to Minidoka a week earlier, and those in Area C had departed on August 18th. Those in Area A, the last of the 7,200 internees quartered at Camp Harmony, would follow on August 22.

Internees, while wrestling with emotions about being uprooted and losing their homes and property, withstood their plight with exceptional fortitude. Camp Harmony on the Puyallup Fairgrounds was located close to the homes they had left behind, so they were somewhat familiar with the area. However, the thought of being uprooted again, without an idea as to where or for how long, was excruciating. Some of the internees broke down and cried.

Separated in different areas for more than four months, internees were happy they would be reunited with family and friends, but their joy was tempered as they were escorted by armed soldiers, as if they were criminals, to the King Street Depot. There they boarded trains for Minidoka, Idaho.

After twenty-seven hours on slow, dusty, creaky trains with shades drawn almost the entire trip, and the only view being the inside of the train, internees were once again ordered by strident soldiers, walking up and down the aisles, to get off the train.

For the first time in more than a day, they were able to see outside. They were shocked at the sight of miles of camelback hills with brown, straggly bushes, so dry and bare in comparison to the rich, green world of Puget Sound. Then they saw a fleet of buses with armed soldiers standing shoulder-to-shoulder beside them. With their guns pointed at the people getting off the train, armed soldiers traced every move as they gave the order.

A half an hour later, they arrived in the desert of Minidoka, Idaho. Barracks still did not have roofs, and there was no hot water. Bulldozers had ground the roads, leaving them inches deep in dust where sagebrush once held down the earth. Stoves had not been installed in many of the units, and temperatures had started to drop at night into the twenties.

From One Prison to Another
The Train Ride

Isseis, Niseis, Sanseis: each family, with
a number issued by the government pinned
to our clothing, we boarded the train at the King Street
Station. Soldiers with rifles, bayonets from muzzles,
followed our movements like hawks.

We were ordered to "keep the shades drawn."
Children looked from the slats between the ends
of the shades and the window panes, eyes appearing
like round black dots. Excited voices—"Oh, there's
a cow, a horse"—accompanied the click-click sound

of the train moving across the tracks. For many, it was
their very first train ride. Older children and adults talked in
soft tones, feeling the weight of moving again to a place
unknown—the future like a black hole. They carried
again their belongings repacked again into the two suitcases.

We rode old trains that the government had pulled
from warehouses, adorned with gas lights and stiff
mohair seats, trains that coughed to sudden halts and creaked.
The air inside: stuffy and stale with no relief.

Grime silting the surfaces of these dilapidated trains
layered the surface of our skin as the diesel engine
creaked its way for thirty hours to our exile:
an American concentration camp in Minidoka.

A sentry holding a rifle, looking out of the guard tower
brought me back to a movie scene: searchlights
moved around 360 degrees. Bright lights like tentacles,
as soldiers with guns waited.

The View

Eyes shadowed with dark lines
were open wide
to hundreds of tar-covered barracks
spread across miles and miles of desolate,
barren land like sheets of postage stamps.

I felt our displacement
    naked one-room quarters,
    cold showers,
    rattlesnakes, scorpions, black widows
    nestled in the rocks and sagebrush.

The mournful howl of coyotes.
Harsh winds blowing sand and dust,
covering our bodies like layers of skin.
Barbed wire wrapped around the camp

Arriving at Minidoka

Hundreds of identical-looking barracks
spread across the barren desert of Minidoka.
The barracks were as primitive as the one-room
quarters of Camp Harmony Assembly Center
on the Puyallup Fairgrounds, the place we had left behind.

Exterior walls were sheathing, black tar paper stretched
over shiplaps where slits appeared in between, where
swirling winds and dust found entry. Insects and bugs
joined in. No interior walls were built, nothing to hold
a brush of paint or wallpaper flowers with a breath of spring.

Shrunken floor boards left open spaces for wind and
dust, also inviting insects into the room. No furniture.
We used our cots to sleep on, as a place to sit, as a desk
to do my homework. Papa built a table and a bench
out of scrap lumber. My handwriting improved.

Knowing the desert was not to be disturbed, the US government
employees still used bulldozers to strip off the natural cover.
Trucks trampled down the grass and churned up the earth.
Our feet sank into mud one inch deep. A slight breeze
lifted dust into suffocating clouds, drifting under doors,

through loose-fitting window sashes, through spaces
in the floors. Unrelenting, unimpeded winds had already
stripped the desert bare. On days when winds were
angry and tumultuous, sand and tiny pebbles, once
protected with a layer of dirt, hurled against us and

against the barracks. We were held prisoners to the spot
where we stood. We covered our eyes and faces
with our hands, burying ourselves inside our jackets
until the winds calmed down, until the winds subsided.

Papa, Block 16 — Mess Hall Cook

Once again, as in those early years
back in the 1920s,
Papa found himself in front of a hot stove.
Instead of a small café, where chairs bumped each other,
open benches formed lines in a mess hall.

Instead of old men with huge appetites,
families, the disinherited, dumped into this forsaken land,
lined up for meals three times each day.

As wind and dust enveloped their bodies
and found their way to any openings.
As biting cold below minus degrees
penetrated to their bones.
As heat reaching 110 degrees
scorched their skins.

They ate on mess hall tables
where a layer of dust was like a chiffon tablecloth
and accompanied meals.

Internees would say,
"We eat dust with our meals."

Papa saw in faces of adults
What children often uttered: "*Ugh.*"

Tripe, tongue, Vienna sausage, Idaho potatoes,
issued by Army Quartermaster Corps
within government allowance,
forty-five cents per day for each internee,
did not suit palates
accustomed to fish and rice flavored with soy sauce.

Internees, backs bent under desert heat,
tended the land with water from the canal.
Fresh vegetables and those pickled
with an oriental flavor
found their way to Block 16 mess hall tables.

I heard voices:
"Our Block 16 cook, Mr. Kato, is improving."

America, Your Country

Papa and I were in our one-room quarters.
"Papa, I volunteered to join the army."

I heard Papa's soft, quivering voice.
"Good, Haruo. America, your country."

Papa made a quick pivot, his back toward my brother and me.
Face hidden.

As he turned around to face us,
we saw tears well in his eyes.
As a child of thirteen, until that moment
I had known only
Papa's smiling and serious face,
never sad.

Much too soon,
army convoys took Haruo and other volunteers
outside the barbed wires.

Memories of my first ice cream soda floated in:
My big brother sat with me
at the Tokuda Drug Store soda fountain
as I enjoyed in slow, slow sips
my very first ice cream soda.

Bubbles that floated on top
also floated inside me.
My young eyes watched Haruo
take money out of his wallet and pay for the ice cream soda
as he chatted with the owner, George Tokuda.

Behind the barbed wires,
I felt the absence of my big brother.

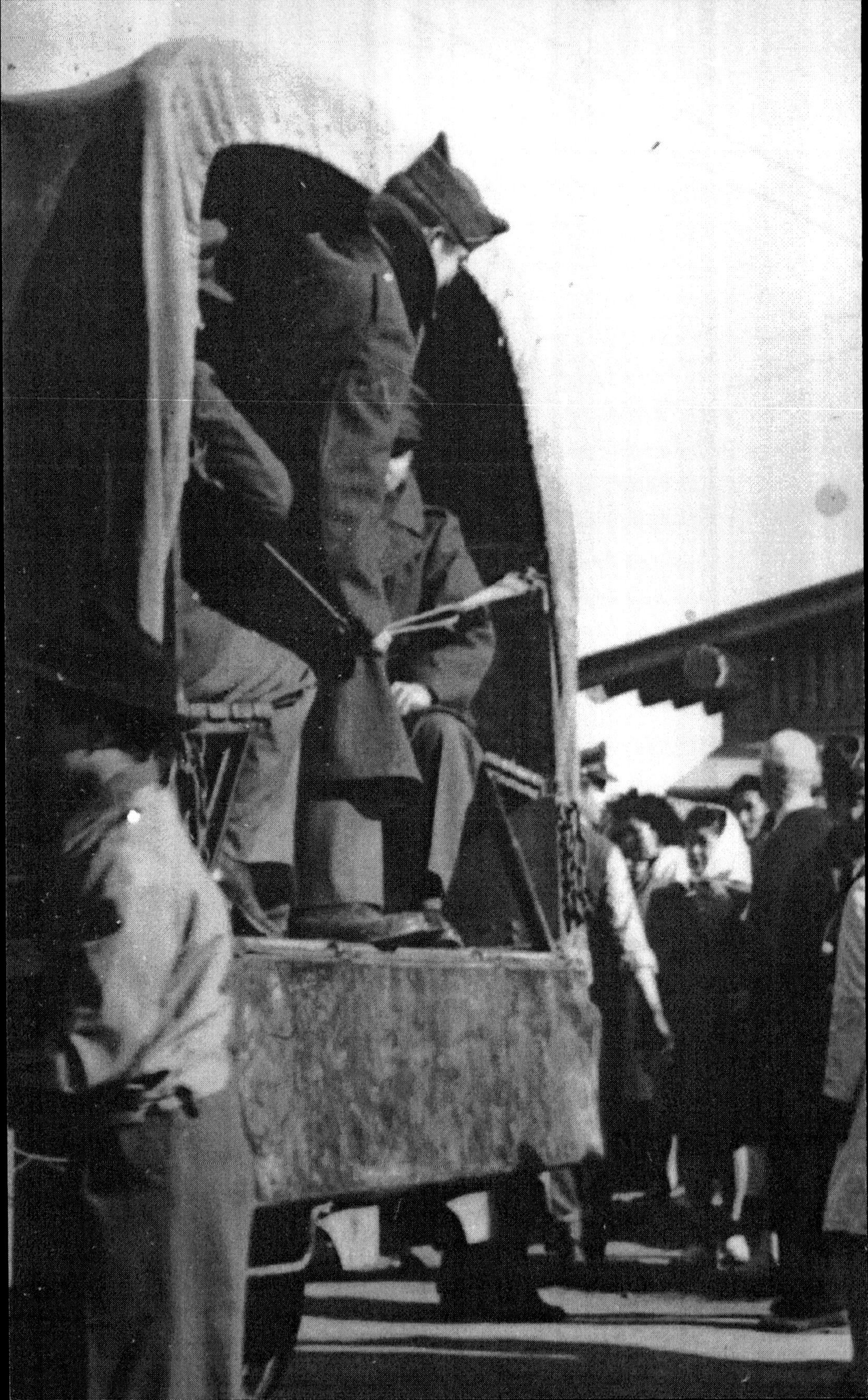

Section VI.

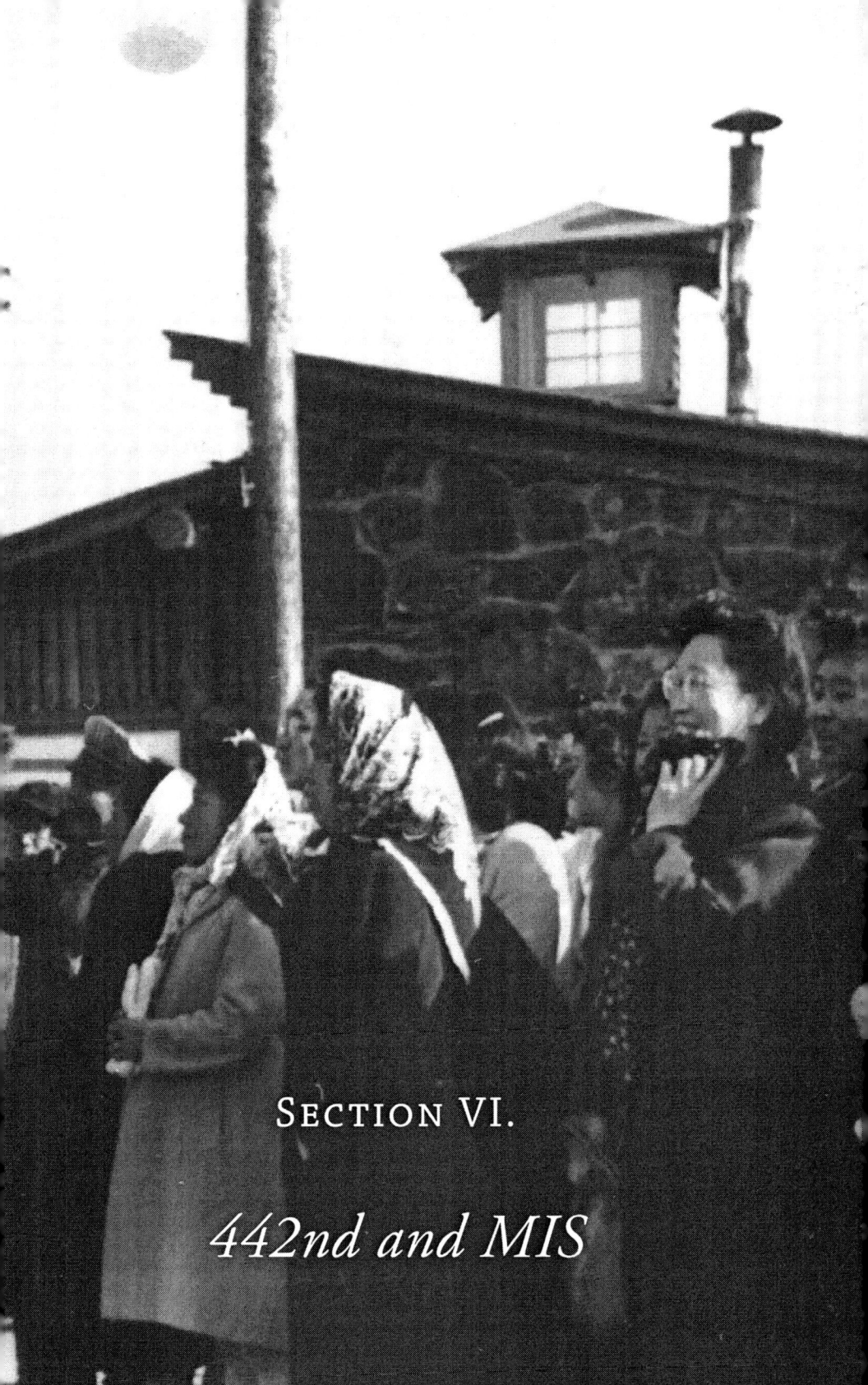

442nd and MIS

Overleaf: Japanese American soldiers leaving Minidoka in a covered army truck while internees wait to say goodbye.
Photo courtesy of the Wing Luke Museum, the Hatate Collection

Nisei Soldiers Dreaming

Nisei soldiers dreamed of voices
who would recognize their valor.

Nisei soldiers' voices were muted,
the ache of their souls carried to their death—

the pain of disenfranchisement
by their own country, covered by earth.

"The most highly decorated combat unit of its size
in United States military history."

"Japanese Americans are loyal American citizens."

Nisei soldiers felt these whispers on the battleground.
They dragged them like shackles on wounded limbs.

Families of Nisei soldiers remain imprisoned
behind the barbed wire of United States concentration camps.

Soldiers in United States Army khakis
like those worn by Nisei soldiers
stood in watchtowers

with guns pointed at Nisei families
while Japanese American soldiers
were fighting our enemy overseas.

Go for Broke

From Anzio to the Po Valley,
from Voges Mountain
to the border of France,
battlegrounds were streaked
with blood.

From Anzio to the Po Valley,
from Voges Mountain
to the border of France,
battlegrounds were wet with tears

from souls pierced by
the barbed wire
that imprisoned them
for their "crime"
of ancestry,

from souls who answered
our nation's call as Americans.
They dragged limbs
on rugged terrain while
being bombarded.

Go for Broke
Go for Broke
echoed above guns
and mortar echoed above
moans of pain

from water-filled foxholes.
They remembered families
at home. They fought
until their bodies
refused to move.

The Same Uniforms

In U.S. Army uniforms, fair-skinned soldiers,
their blonde and auburn hair
highlighted by the rays of desert sun,
stood in watchtowers with machine guns
pointed at families of Nisei solders
who were wearing US Army uniforms,
fighting on the battlegrounds overseas.

Families of the Nisei soldiers felt the irony
as they tipped their heads and looked upward
at the soldier in the watchtower
pointing the machine gun toward them
inside the barbed wire of Minidoka.

As the Nisei soldiers fought, they imagined
gates to the concentration camps opening:
fathers, mothers, brothers, and sisters
each with two suitcases, exiting.

America's Supreme Secret Weapon

Concealed from the public,
like blueprints of the atomic bombs,
US government kept them buried in secrecy,
Japanese American soldiers in the Pacific,
who used their language and knowledge of their ancestry.

Nisei soldiers of the Military Intelligence Service
decoded military secrets
written in Japanese characters and
listened over the wires to voices of men.

who had the same folds in their eyes,
with skin the same hue,
and with surnames identical to their own.

They served as the eyes and ears of the Allied Pacific Forces.

General Willoughby said:
"The 6,000 Niseis shortened the war
in the Pacific by two years."

President Truman said of these linguists,
"They are our human secret weapons."

Yet only one Nisei had been awarded
the Congressional Medal of Honor.
Seen through the lens of racism,
their fervent American souls were blurred.

American Heroes

William Nakamura left his desk vacant
at the University of Washington;
James Okubo left his desk vacant
at Western Washington University.

Paragraphs unfinished on term papers,
math problems still to be completed,
their educations halted,
William and James were forced to leave.

William saw his father's face,
his mouth turned downward, eyes moistened
for the loss of his wife who died one month before.
for the loss of a lifetime of toil.

William Nakamura, his brother, and sisters
faced emotions biting and unfamiliar.

James Okubo, with his mother, father, two brothers, two sisters,
two orphaned nephews, and two nieces,
left Bellingham for Pinedale Assembly Center, California.

James's mama and papa closed the door to their restaurant
that fed and clothed nine children.
They left behind the stove where meals were cooked,
booths where people sat and ate.

With the absence of five boys,
quarters of the Okubo family
in the Heart Mountain Internment Camp
felt empty.

They took with them to the battlegrounds
the voices of their fathers.
"Bring honor to yourselves,
your family, and your country."

They dragged the weight of a
soldier's uniform, US government issue,
same as those worn by soldiers
pointing guns at members of their families.

For their heroics on the battlefield,
William K. Nakamura was awarded the Distinguished Service Cross,
and James Okubo was awarded the Silver Star.

Haruo Returns to Seattle

Mama's voice wraps around Haruo:
"Kaette kureta. Kaette kureta."
(You have come home. You have come home.)

Mama's and Papa's eyes trace
his face like a road map.

They see in his eyes, a soldier of Company E,
442nd Infantry Unit, battlegrounds across Europe,
rescue of the Lost Battalion.

His eyes holding ravages of war and lost comrades,
replacing those youthful eyes filled with hope when
he answered his nation's call from behind the barbed
wire gates of Minidoka.

Papa and Mama notice his firmer chin,
the deeper lines, broader shoulders.

Haruo hears Mama repeating, "Arigatai, arigatai."
(I am thankful, I am thankful.)
He sees Mama's and Papa's shoulders
now yielding to their age,
a burden of starting all over again,
after suffering a loss of a lifetime.

He hears their once strong voices hesitant,
wavering, and uncertain.
He sees his family experiencing a different Minidoka.
Graffiti throughout the city reads, *Go Back—we don't want Japs.*
Stares say, "Why did you come back?"

There are no automobiles for $20 like the one Haruo sold.
We sit in transit buses that move us across the town.

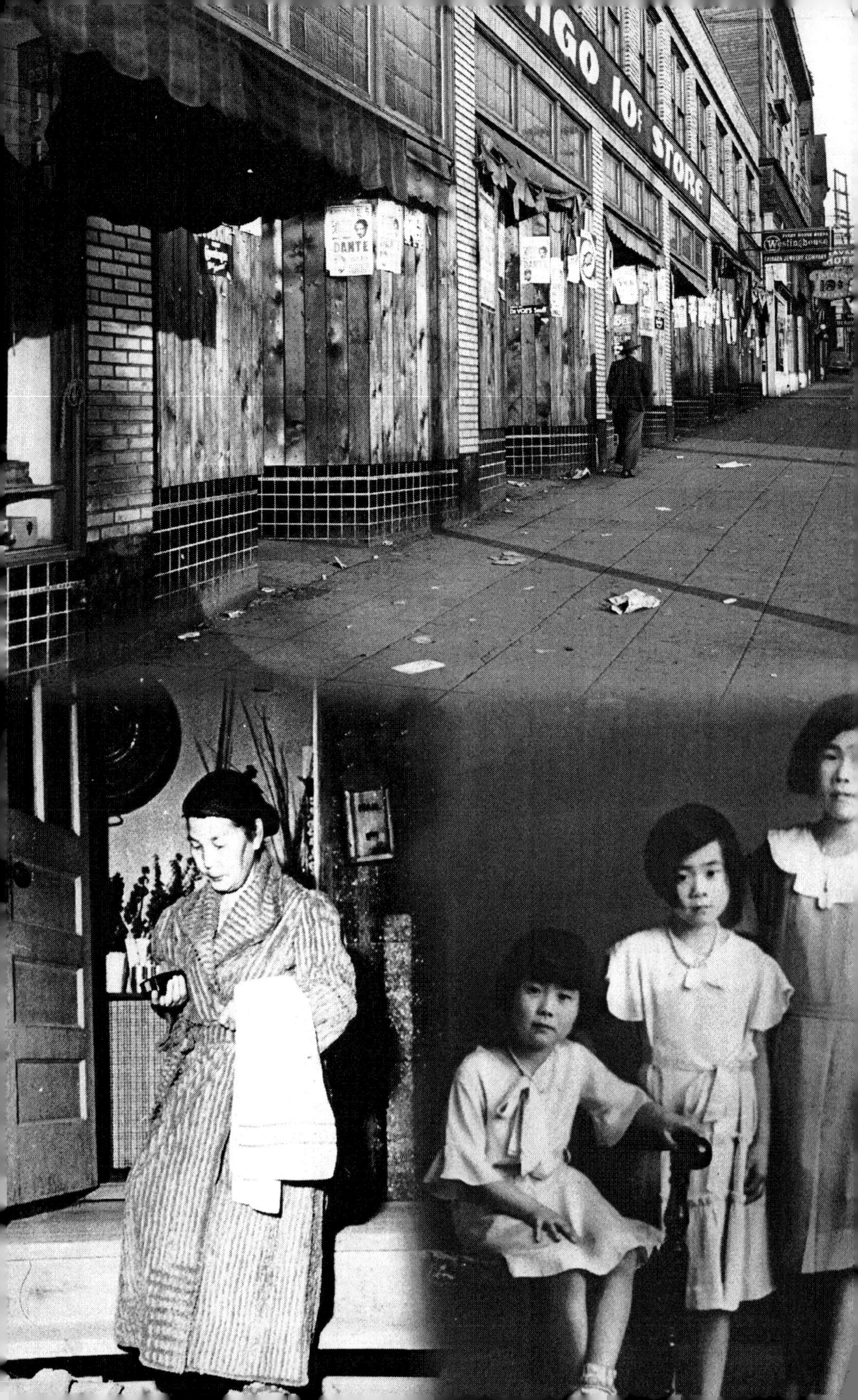
10¢ STORE
DANTE
DANTE
Westinghouse

Section VII.

Looking Back

Overleaf left, top: The Higo Ten-Cent Store, located on Jackson Street, after the evacuation. The Murakamis were able to reopen their store after the war because they were able to pay property taxes while interned.
Photo courtesy of the Museum of History & Industry

Overleaf left, bottom left: Issei woman leaving the barracks to shower at the communal washing facility.
Photo courtesy of the Wing Luke Museum

Overleaf left, bottom right: The Kato sisters, left to right, Suma, Aki, Fusae.
Photo courtesy of the Kurose Family Collection

Overleaf right, top: Internees waiting in line for a meal outside of the mess hall.
Photo courtesy of the Museum of History & Industry, Seattle Post-Intelligencer Collection

Overleaf right, bottom: Two children (Irene and Hiroshi Ito) playing between barracks in the Minidoka concentration camp.
Photo courtesy of the Wing Luke Museum, the Hatate Collection

Wounds Still Open

1.

Voices hushed,
Wounds fresh.

Today, thirty-nine years later,
    dramas unfold
      in newsprint,
      in redress meetings,
      in writings.

Words, like pitchforks,
    unearthing what has been buried
      in the folds of gray matter,
      deeper in souls.

Tears replaced giggles.

The child of fourteen discovered:

Her citizenship was hidden
in the folds of her eyelids
and under her skin.

Her voice resounding, "God bless America, land that I love,"
was not in tune.

Her voice declaring,
"I pledge allegiance to the flag
of the United States of America,"
was not heard.

Unlike other children's,
hers was a different pitch, buried in Japanese ancestry.

Bubbles effervescing
    inside her heart
    as she sang the "Star-Spangled Banner,"
    were invisible on the outside.

The Bill of Rights and the Constitution
were not irrevocable promises and mandates.
    They were colorful,
    striped,
    rhetorical.

2.

Piercing edges of barbed wire,
guns carried by soldiers
who peered down
from the watchtower
imprisoned her.

Army-issued cots lined up in a row
rubbed against each other in the open room.
She could not separate her breathing
from others' in her family.

She remembers

How she longed for the toilet like the one left behind.
      the one and a half blocks
      to the community latrine
      stretched into miles
      at night
      in the snow
      in the cold.

      Swollen bladders
      pushed heavy eyelids
      and opened doors
      put heavy clothing over pajamas.

How she longed for privacy behind doors.

There was only one door
      leading outside in their barrack.
No doors in the crowded latrines,
no curtains around community showers.

How she longed for the kitchen at home.

Mama's cooking sent urgings to her stomach.
She felt warmth around the big round table.

The mess hall cook whacked an aluminum pan
with a large metal spoon.
The clang clang clang brought people from their cots.

They formed long lines in front of the mess halls
      for meals served three times each day,
      fighting wind and dust,
      biting cold,
      scorching heat.

      Children sat by other children,
      parents with other parents,
      girlfriends with boyfriends,
      boyfriends with girlfriends.

How she longed for the washing machine at home,
squeezing and hugging the wash.

Metal washboards in the community laundry room
      were rigid, scraping knuckles,
      making them tender and sore.

How she longed for double-decker ice cream cones.

The Idaho sun made our lips dry.
There were no confectioneries.

Her papa's $12 monthly salary,
as the mess hall cook, would not stretch.

> Papa spent the money at the block canteen:
> toothpaste and toothbrushes,
> cream for chapped faces and hands,
> thread for sewing and mending small clothing items
> for members of the family.

She Remembers:

Wailing of babies.
Voices escaped through thin walls of barracks.
> Their pleadings reached down to her feet.
> Mothers cried by their babies silently.
> No running water.
> No refrigerator.

Milk turned into lumps
> from the heat of summer,
> from heat of pot-bellied stove,
> in the one-room quarters.

The community latrine was an almost-two-block walk.
Diapers had to be rinsed in chamber pots.

A whole year had passed since Executive Order 9066
forced her to leave her home.

She turned fifteen:
      no birthday cake,
      but bubbles floated inside her.

Boys made her giggle.
      She noticed them by basketball hoops,
      no longer just part of the post;
      they had voices
      that made her face warm.

3.

Nisei men filed their IV-C (enemy alien) card
in the folds of their wallets,
leaving its weight in their back pockets.

Almost three hundred young men volunteered from
the Minidoka Internment Camp.

On the day of departure,
>	barracks emptied and
>	roads leading to the gates were dotted with people.
>	For the elderly and very young,
>	the three-mile walk
>	from one end of the camp
>	to the gates
>	stretched to endless miles.

Not even on this day
did the sun hold back
or the wind
blow more gently.

The temperature was in the 100s.
>	Wind twisted and turned,
>	turning the desert sand
>	to a fine spray,
>	then to a thousand darting needles,
>	holding people prisoner.

The usual scene by the gates of Minidoka was transformed.

>	Along the flag post,
>	dozens of army convoys
>	waited to take volunteers
>	outside the barbed wire fence.

The almost ten thousand inhabitants
        shook hands,
        hugged,
        and cried.

The air was interrupted.

"Take care of yourself, Mama."
"Take care of yourself, Papa."
"We'll miss you."
"I love you."
"Be sure to write."
"Shikkari, shikkari (be brave, bear up)."

Army convoys stirred the temperamental desert floor,
        creating its own dust bowl,
        competing with Minidoka's.

Gates closed on the last convoy,
the sobbing competed against the drone of wheels.

4.

Loneliness swept the camp like a plague.
Absence of the young men was felt from

       barracks quarters
       block mess halls
       community latrines
       community showers
       dusty roads.

News of staggering casualties
among the combat team
came through the barbed wire.

For the first time in her life,
she encountered
the sting of death.

Two young men—Francis Kinoshita
       and Yoshio Kato—
          were among those killed in action
          on the battlefields of Europe.
The quarters they left behind
were in "Block 16," like hers.

She felt the devotion and valor
of the 442nd Regimental Combat Team.
They took the greatest casualties
and earned the highest distinction.

But there were no fancy, fragrant flowers for memorial services.
The sagebrush blossoms hid in their plainness.

5.

Against the patter of heavy rains,
drenched Nisei soldiers
stood like fence posts.

Eyes fixed,
ears opened
to the voice of President Truman
on the lawn of the White House:

"You fought not only your enemy,
but you fought prejudice and you won.
Keep up that fight, and we will continue
to win to make this great republic stand
for what the Constitution says it stands for."

These words were salve
to wounded souls of Nisei soldiers.

These same words fell like thunder
on ears of anti-Japanese Americans.
"American Japs may fight in Europe,
but you'll never get them to fight
in the Pacific against Japan."

"We'll prove our loyalty to the United States,"
became each soldier's mantra,
resonating within his soul.

Nisei soldiers removed the bondage of families
in the ten concentration camps,
located in deserts throughout the United States.

Again, she is hearing some voices:
"Look what Japan did."

Her citizenship
lies hidden
in the folds of her eyes,
under her skin.

Citizenship behind the Steel Door

United States naturalization laws
had two doors:
One, swinging freely on hinges,
welcomed European immigrants
inside.

The other,
immovable, hinges rusted,
closed, kept Japanese immigrants
outside.

At age seventeen, Papa had come from Japan.
Later this was the inscription on Papa's tombstone:
1888–1951

In 1952,
the steel door was pried open.
For Papa, it was too late.

Niseis went to Congress,
bringing their pleas:
"Open the door, let their parents, the Isseis, inside the steel door."

Ten years later Congress, yielding to their voice,
Allowed citizenship to parents of Japanese Americans,
for the first time in 162 years.

But for so many
the American Dream
remained an impossible dream.

Backs were now bent with age,
hands gnarled,
eyesight and memory diminished.

For those with the American Dream within their reach
a legacy of toil and endurance continued.

Their tired limbs
often needed support of canes and wheelchairs.

Their once sharp minds
had lost the keenness of their earlier years.

They waited for rides to their classes.
Notebooks felt heavy with their determination.

They asked instructors

"Yukkuri hanashi de kudasai"
(Please talk slowly).
"Mata Mata yutte kudasai"
 (Please repeat. Please repeat).
Heads were bent over pages during daylight and by lamplight.

The constitutional amendments recited with a Japanese accent
in sing-song cadence
resonated in homes
over a period of months.

They stood before federal judges,
eyes open wide,
souls smiling,
Taking the oath of allegiance
as American citizens.

Tribute to Our Isseis

Their footprints have long been erased by the
shifting sands, yet our feet feel the indelible
indentations that they left behind.

On upright shoulders, the Issei silently bore
The enormity of Executive Order 9066,
which stole their lifelong dreams
and imprisoned them in a U.S. concentration camp.

Kodomo no tame (for the sake of their children),
the Issei left their legacy of *shikataganai* (it cannot be helped),
gaman (persevere), *shikkari* (endure), *giri* (obligation),
echoing in the winds of Minidoka.

They endured the loss of sons, proud soldiers of the
442nd Regimental Combat Team, who distinguished
themselves as the most highly decorated combat unit,
suffering the most casualties for a military unit of its size.

They suffered during the absence of sons and daughters
who served as linguists in the Military Intelligence Service,
decoding military secrets, serving as the eyes and ears
of the Allied Pacific Forces, American's secret weapon
against the Japanese.
General MacArthur said they shortened the war by at least two
years.

With upright shoulders, the Issei attended memorial services for sons killed in action.
U.S. soldiers wearing the same uniforms stood in watchtowers,
with guns pointing at their families.
The Issei sat on folding chairs behind barbed wire.

Shikataganai, gaman, shikari, giri
echoes over miles and miles of barren land
under the harsh desert winds of Minidoka.

The Legacy of Lights Out

While rays of sun filter through the window
and warm my shoulders, I have my fingers, some
gnarled with arthritis, on the computer keyboard.
I revisit the "curfew—lights out" regulation of 1942.

I relive those moments as a child when I would sleep
through the night while my parents groped
their way in complete darkness between six cots
squeezed together in an eighteen-by-twenty foot space.
They inched their way toward the entrance,

reaching and feeling the door knob, twisting it open,
then stepping outside, walking to the community
outhouse on dimly lit muddy walkways, then returning
to their one-room quarters, sheathed in complete
darkness. They felt their way to the cots, using

their hands like surgeons over the muslin bags,
feeling bumps and valleys formed by the straw,
then laying their bodies on top of the cots.
Sticks of straw poked them throughout the night.
Through the thin walls dividing the rooms,

I recall hearing the cries of babies, but as a child
of fourteen sleeping through the night,
I was unaware of mothers in complete
darkness, changing soiled diapers, fastening
and unfastening safety pins while their babies

tossed and turned, kicking their feet like restless
colts. I didn't see the mothers in the middle of the night,
trying to soothe their fussy children
crying for cups of water. There were no faucets
in their one-room quarters. Mothers were required
to get written permission to turn on the light to give

medicine for their very sick children. I feel the weight
of these restrictions and the tears that flowed from the eyes
of mothers clothed in darkness.

I Thank Aki for Scolding Me

"Put your poetry in a book."

Aki started way back when we were children, making friends
while my sister Fuzzy (Fusaye) and I did the chores
that she should have been doing.

As we faced a sink full of dishes
or dusted the apartment rails,
we'd ask "Where's Aki?
Where did she go?"

She'd always manage to slip out of the house
"for more important things" in Aki's mind.
Mama would say, "Komaru ne komaru ne."
(In English, one might say
Mama was at her wit's end.)

We'd find Aki's photograph
in the newspapers
amidst a sea of people
marching for different causes.

Aki, you couldn't miss.
She looked like a kid.
Her 4'10" stature
stood out among the rest.

Instead of being embarrassed,
I should have been proud,

But the voice within me then
Was strong:

"These are not the things
Nisei women should do.
Oh! This radical sister of mine."

But as I grew older
I saw things differently.

I learned to understand what courage really is.
I saw Aki's activism, her energy, her tenacity, her theme of peace,
her belief in human rights,
her love of science,
her love of teaching.

Two peace gardens dedicated to her, a science fair
proclamation in her name:
a day,
a week
a month,
even a century.

The First Poems

My children had left the nest:
three had acquired their degrees at the University of Washington,
the fourth just accepted to its school of dentistry.
I felt free to fly.
I enrolled in a writing class
through the university's distance learning program.

I sought to capture my passion on paper:
the beauty of majestic mountains,
crystalline lakes, flora-covered earth,
sunsets and sunrises, the inhumanity of man, footprints of war.
My passion to urge compassion and change
was like a pilot light inside me.

And then the professor gave a writing assignment:
a personal experience connected to a historical event.
I had a mistaken notion that
to write poetry was to keep with poetic subjects.

Instead of what I thought was poetry,
I found images of Executive Order 9066
posted to telephone poles,
personal belongings in boxes
left in rooms emptied of their families.

I found families carrying two suitcases, departing on buses.
I found barbed wire, mess halls, community latrines,

soldiers with rifles pointed at families from guard towers.
I found my brother leaving for the American war
from the American internment camp.

Tears flowed and my papers were
crushed and thrown—a pile in the wastepaper basket.

As teenagers, my children learned for the first time
that my family was one of those incarcerated in an American internment camp
because of our Japanese ancestry.

My body shook.
Images of a girl, fourteen years old,
locked inside; my soul
opened and became my composition.

Notes

Overleaf, top: Racial epithet written on a garage in Seattle.
Photo courtesy of the Museum of History & Industry, Seattle Post-Intelligencer Collection

Overleaf, bottom: Internees stuffing straw into cloth bags for use as mattresses. (Photo taken at the Colorado River Relocation Center.)
Photo courtesy of the National Archives and Records Administration

The Early Years

What was an everyday experience for the Nisei generation is an anomaly for our children. With the population of Issei women disappearing, no longer is the scenario of women bowing, resembling pigeons, a familiar one. Whenever or wherever Issei women met—in public or private—they greeted each other with a bow, following a custom they had learned in Japan. A shallow bow, with a slight bend at the waist and head lowered very briefly, was equivalent to a hello—an informal greeting. In contrast, a deeper bow, bending the head lower and keeping the head bent, and repeating it, showed more respect and could be an expression of appreciation, embarrassment, condolence, or apology. Nisei children often felt embarrassed about the custom of their parents.

From the second grade through the eighth grade, I attended Washington School, located on Eighteenth Avenue and Main Street in Seattle. Mr. Sears, the principal, was a man not inclined toward change. As far back as I can recall, he wore the same striped navy blue suit, and his heavy crop of gray hair always seemed to be ruffled and in need of combing.

At the start of each day, we would gather in the hallway, all crowded together. Without exception, he greeted the students with a thunderous "Good morning, boys and girls!" He expected the complete participation of every student in a response, equally whopping and enthusiastic. Whenever he felt the response was lacking, he would say, "Let's try again," and would cup his hand to his ears. Mr. Sears's greeting was always followed by the flag salute, the Pledge of Allegiance, and the singing of "My Country 'Tis of Thee."

I remember rattling off the Pledge of Allegiance with the rest of the students, but as I grew older, the Pledge of Allegiance was my personal declaration of devotion, accompanied by feelings of love, conviction, and loyalty to my country. I often noticed a lump in my throat as I spoke these words: "I pledge allegiance to the Flag of the United States of America, and to the Republic for which it stands, one nation indivisible, with liberty and justice for all." I remember feeling: *How exciting it is to be a part of the American dream. How fortunate that my parents immigrated to America from Japan.*

During my primary years, the colors—red, white, and blue—were merely some lines arranged on a cloth with stars at the upper left-hand corner. As I advanced into the higher grades, the fabric symbolized the Bill of Rights and democracy—our American heritage.

December 7, 1941

"Another Day of Infamy"

The bombing of Pearl Harbor led to hysteria, fueled by those anxious to see the Japanese people removed from their community. Motivated by racial animus and by the prospect for financial gain, they pressured the government to remove people of Japanese ancestry from the West Coast. Congress acted and on February 19, 1942, President Roosevelt signed Executive Order 9066.

> *NOW, THEREFORE, by virtue of the authority vested in me as President of the United States, and Commander-in-Chief of the Army and Navy, I hereby authorize and direct the Secretary of War, and the Military Commanders whom he may from time to time designate or any designated Commander deems such action necessary or desirable, to prescribe military areas in such place and of such extent as he or the appropriate Military Commander may determine, from which any or all persons may be excluded, and with respect to which, the right of any person to enter, remain in, or leave shall be subject to whatever restrictions the Secretary of War or the appropriate Military Commander may impose in his discretion...*

The day after EO 9066 was signed into law, John DeWitt, the Commander of Western Defense Command, received a directive from the secretary of War Henry Stimson, and a memo from the Assistant Secretary of War, John McCloy ordering him to remove certain classes of West Coast residents.

The memo from McCloy to DeWitt categorized West Coast residents into six classes:

Class 1: Japanese aliens

Class 2: American citizens of Japanese lineage

Class 3: German aliens

Class 4: Italian aliens

Class 5: Any persons, whether citizens or aliens, who are suspected for any reason by you or your responsible subordinates of being actually or potentially dangerous either as saboteurs, espionage agents, fifth columnists or subversive persons.

Class 6: All other persons who are or who may be within the Western Defense Command.

American citizens of Japanese ancestry were deemed more dangerous than German and Italian aliens, and for practical considerations, only Japanese aliens and American citizens of Japanese lineage were ordered to be excluded en masse from the West Coast.

Signs by the Western Defense Command and Fourth Army Wartime Civil Control Administration were nailed to telephone posts and bulletin boards throughout the city. They read:

Instructions to All Persons of Japanese Ancestry

To those living in the following area: **All** that portion of the City of Seattle, State of Washington, lying generally south of an east-west line at which Jackson Street meets Elliott Bay; thence easterly along Jackson Street to Fifth Avenue; thence southerly on Fifth Avenue to Dearborn Street; thence easterly to Dearborn Street to Twenty-third Avenue; thence northerly on Twenty-third Avenue to Yesler Way; thence easterly on Yesler Way to Lake Washington.

Pursuant to the provisions of Civilian Exclusion Order No. 18, this Headquarters, dated April 24, 1942, all persons of Japanese ancestry, both alien and non-alien, will be evacuated from the above area by 11 o'clock noon, P.W.T., Friday, May 1, 1942.

Evacuees must carry with them on departure for the Assembly Center, the following property:

(a) Bedding and linens (no mattress) for each member of the family

(b) Toilet articles for each member of the family

(c) Extra clothing for each member of the family

(d) Sufficient knives, forks, spoons, plates, bowls, and cups for each member of the family

(e) Essential personal effects for each member of the family

The size and number of packages is limited to that which can be carried by individual or family members. No pets of any kind will be permitted.

"Camp Harmony"

On August 20, 1942, those confined in Area B were escorted by armed soldiers to a large area of the fairgrounds where a fleet of buses awaited. Evacuees confined to Area D had already been sent to Minidoka a week earlier, and those in Area C had departed on the eighteenth. Those in Area A, the last of the 7,200 internees quartered at Camp Harmony, our earlier concentration camp, would follow on August 22.

Minidoka

Minidoka was located near the town of Twin Falls, Idaho on Bureau of Reclamation land. Situated at an elevation of 3,800 feet, the climate was semi-arid with temperature extremes reaching minus 30 degree to 104 degrees Fahrenheit. Only about 25 percent of the sagebrush desert was suitable for cultivation, but the soil between the lava outcroppings was fertile if provided with irrigation. The Bureau of Reclamation had initiated development of the public land by building a series of dams and canals on the Snake River. Canals were built using labor from the Civilian Conservation Corps in the 1930s. Evacuees at Minidoka worked on maintaining the canals and provided labor to clear the land and put several thousand acres under cultivation. Most of the food needed for Minidoka and perhaps a surplus for other relocation centers was produced here. Major crops were potatoes, beans, and onions, along with feed crops such as alfalfa, clover, barley and oats. After the war, the land reverted to the Bureau of Reclamation and was made available for settlement to returning Veterans.

442nd and MIS

American men of Japanese ancestry who had been classified 1-A (eligible for immediate induction) were reclassified to IV-F (ineligible for induction) and later reclassified to IV-C (enemy alien) by local draft boards. Later, Classification IV-C was revoked by the War Department. The men in the concentration camps received the news that a special classification was created for Japanese-Americans.

President Franklin Delano Roosevelt declared: "The proposal of the War Department to organize a combat team consisting of loyal American citizens of Japanese descent has my full approval. No loyal citizen of the United States should be denied the democratic right to exercise the responsibilities of his citizenship regardless of his ancestry. The principle on which this country was founded and by which it has always been governed is that Americanism is a matter of the heart and mind; Americanism is not and never was a matter of race or ancestry."

"The Lost Battalion"

With only two days' rest, the 100/442nd was called upon to rescue the so-called Lost Battalion, of the 36th Infantry Division which had been cut off by German forces. After two rescue attempts by the 36th Division, the Lost Battalion had been isolated almost a week, was low on food and ammunition, and was in very grave danger. Although the 100th/442nd was at only half strength, the unit fought four of the bloodiest and fiercest days of the war, which resulted in more than 800 casualties to rescue the 211 men of the Lost Battalion. In gratitude several years after the war, Texas Governor John Connolly officially proclaimed all former members of the 100th/442nd Honorary Texans.

In early March 1945, General Mark Clark personally requested the return of the 100th/442nd to Italy to create a diversionary attack on the western end of the German Gothic Line, which had withstood six months of Allied Army efforts. In the predawn hours of April 5, 1945, three battalions of the 100th/442nd silently climbed the sheer faces of steep mountains cliffs in total darkness. At 5:00 a.m., after an artillery barrage, they successfully overtook the surprised German defenders, and in just 32 minutes broke the unbreakable Gothic Line. Their advance continued from the mountains just north of Azzano, past Massa, Carrara, the shore guns at LaSpezia, Genoa and into Aulla and the Po Valley, This diversionary attack became the key, final offensive that ended the war in Italy in May 1945.

In an ironic twist of fate, Nisei soldiers from the 522nd Field Artillery Battalion of the 442nd—soldiers whose families were still imprisoned by their own government in concentration camps back in America—liberated survivors from Hitler's notorious Dachau death camp near Munich, Germany.

Captain Masao Yamada wrote, "My heart weeps for our men. I am probably getting too soft, but to me the price is too costly for our men. I feel this way more because the burden is laid on the combat team when the rest of the 141st Division is not forced to take responsibility. When we complete this mission, we will have written with our own blood another chapter in the story of our adventures in Democracy."

The 442nd infantry unit was the most highly decorated combat team of its size in United States military history.

7   Presidential Unit Citations

21 Medals of Honor

33 Distinguished Service Crosses

1   Distinguished Service Medal

559 Silver Stars, plus 28 Oak Leaf Clusters

22 Legions of Merit

15 Soldiers' Medals

4,000 Bronze Stars, plus 1,200 Oak Leaf Clusters

9,486 Purple Hearts

2   Meritorious Unit Service Plaques

36 Army Commendations

87 Division Commendations

19 decorations from Allied nations

A special plaque of appreciation from the Texans of the Lost Battalion.

This is one of many poems dedicated to 442nd Regimental Combat Team by James M. Hanley, who was one of the senior commanders of the 442nd Regimental Combat Team.

What should we as Americans say of the Nisei
This is what we should say
We should highly resolve
That the dead shall not have died in vain
That the Japanese American sacrifices
Shall not be lost in the mists of time
That this nation shall have a new Birth of Freedom
And shall develop racial ethnic and religious
Bonds of harmony and
We shall revere this Government
Of the People By the People For the People.

"America's Supreme Secret Weapon"

Approximately six thousand Nisei men and women served in the US Military Intelligence Service (MIS) during World War II and fought covertly against the land of their ancestry, contributing tremendously to the Allied victory in the Pacific. They were America's supreme secret weapon, and their activities have been one of the best-kept secrets of the war.

The Nisei in the MIS were indispensable and irreplaceable, because of their knowledge of the Japanese language, which few on the Allied side could understand. They served side by side with Allied forces in all campaigns and on all fronts throughout the Pacific in China, India, Burma and in Europe.

Nisei members of the MIS laboriously translated millions of captured documents—maps, battle plans, diaries, letters, records, manuals—producing extensive intelligence that influenced Allied strategy and operations. They also interrogated prisoners, and on occasion persuaded enemy soldiers to surrender. Because of the intelligence provided by the nisei in the MIS, the U.S. Army knew more about its enemy prior to battles during the Pacific campaign than ever before in history. MIS soldiers were deemed so valuable to Major General Frank Merrill that he ordered his troops to protect them with their own lives. Major General Charles Willoughby, Chief of Intelligence for General Douglas MacArthur, said: "6000 Nisei soldiers saved a million lives and shortened the war in the Pacific by two years."

"America Heroes"

July 4, 1944

Private First Class William Kenzo Nakamura's platoon became pinned down, near Castellina, Italy, by enemy machine gun fire from a concealed position. Private First Class William Nakamura crawled twenty yards on all fours toward the hostile nest of gunfire, he raised himself to a kneeling position and threw four hand grenades, killing at least three of the enemy soldiers.

Enemy weapons silenced, William crawled back to his platoon, enabling them to advance. Later his company was ordered to withdraw so that mortar barrage could be placed on the ridge. William remained in position to cover his comrades' withdrawal. While moving toward the safety of a wooded draw, his platoon became pinned down by deadly machine-gun fire. William crawled to a point from which he could fire on the enemy position. He fired his weapon, pinning down the enemy's machine gunners. His platoon was then able to withdraw to safety, without suffering further casualties. Private First Class Nakamura was killed during this heroic stand. In another location not too far away, William's brother was also killed on the battlefield near Biffontaine, France.

October 28, 1944

Technician Fifth Grade James Okubo, above the thunderous sound of mortar heard voices of comrades crying "Medic! Medic! Under constant enemy fire, dodging grenades hurled at him, James Okubo crawled like an angleworm, scraping the surface of the French forest that pulled and tore his clothing and gouged his skin. Technician Okubo treated seventeen men who had been badly wounded, followed by eight more on October 29.

November 4, 1944

Running seventy-five yards, almost the length of a football field,. James Okubo answered the cry of a badly wounded soldier trapped in a burning tank. Dodging the hail of gunfire, he climbed into the tank, still holding the heat of fire, emitting smoke and choking from the smell of burnt metal. James lifted the man on his back, like a hundred-pound sack of rice, carrying him to safety. James Okubo was awarded the Silver Star.

On a battlefield not too far away, two brothers of James Okubo, Sumi and Hiram, also with the 442nd Regimental Combat Team, were injured and disabled. Cousin Isamu Kunimatsu, raised with the Okubo family, was killed on the battlefield in Italy. James Okubo's father passed away in the Heart Mountain Internment Camp while James was caring for the wounded on the battlefield in Europe.

June 21, 2000

William K. Nakamura was among the twenty Japanese Americans soldiers with a Distinguished Service Cross upgraded to Congressional Medal of Honor posthumously.

James Okubo's Silver Star was upgraded to Congressional Medal of Honor.

November 9, 2000

President William Jefferson Clinton signed a bill to name the federal courthouse in Seattle, Washington, in honor of Private First Class William Kenzo Nakamura, recipient of the Congressional Medal of Honor, posthumously. On the same day, the National Japanese American Memorial was dedicated in Washington, D.C.

Attorney General Janet Reno read a letter from President William Jefferson Clinton: "We are diminished when any American is targeted unfairly because of his or her heritage. This memorial and the internment sites are powerful reminders that stereotyping, discrimination, hatred, and racism have no place in this country."

March 26, 2001

The Federal General Service Administration held a ceremony naming the federal courthouse in Seattle, Washington, after William K. Nakamura.

February 21, 2002

Almost three hundred people came together for the dedication ceremony of the Technician Fifth Grade James K. Okubo Medical Center. At the dedication, United States General Eric Shinseki stated, "Let me depart from protocol a bit and mention by name George Yamane and Steve Finley, without whose instincts and determination about doing what is right this ceremony would not have happened, and our nation and the army would have missed a wonderful opportunity to recognize this great soldier and patriot."

This medical complex will be more than a tribute to a great soldier and patriot. It will tell volumes more: It will carry the story of a part of American history that has been left out of history books for more than half a century, about the 120,000 Japanese, including citizens like James Okubo, who were dislocated into internment camps on the basis of ancestry. It will also be a story of valor and patriotism of Nisei soldiers who fought to defend their country in its moment of peril despite their families' and their own loss of freedom.

United States Army Chief of Staff General Eric Shinseki in his keynote address stated:

"There is no one more deserving of this recognition, no one whose name could be more appropriate for this facility, a medical and dental complex in this great state, on this great army post, no name more fitting than James K. Okubo's. We must share his story ... pass on the legacy of service to future generations, and inspire in them the desire to add their own page to our country's and the AJA (Americans of Japanese ancestry) community's history of honor and service.

"It is our responsibility; our children need and want to know these stories and such examples of selflessness will sustain us in the years, and the crises, which lay ahead."

I found these words resonating inside me.

Looking Back

"Wounds Still Open"

Feelings of apprehension and discomfort were heightened as the days grew closer to December 7. This year marked the fiftieth anniversary of newspaper headlines, radio announcements, and TV broadcasts declaring "JAPAN BOMBS PEARL HARBOR." I felt fearful that unresolved suspicion and hate would be resurrected against Niseis. The graphic scenes played over and over would open old wounds. The role of the Niseis in the Military Intelligence Service was still the best-kept secret;

this fact kept gnawing at me. If we Niseis did not raise our voices, how would the public to know?

"Citizenship behind the Steel Door"

Isseis learned the different branches of government and their functions. They learned words: *amendments, constitution, liberty, citizenship, rights,* and *freedom.* They learned their meaning in the context of the Constitution and Bill of Rights, denied their children that put them behind barbed wires, in United States concentration camps, purely on the basis of their Japanese ancestry. Isseis never raised the question.

"Government Regulation"

Part XXXV, WCCA Operations Manual

[At 9:30 p.m. each evening a person made a door-to-door check to make surewe were observing the nine o'clock curfew and that we followed the government regulations.]

All radios and lights of every kind in all evacuees' quarters shall be turned off by occupants not later than 10:30 p.m. Lights shall remain off throughout the hours of darkness. Exceptions to lighting regulations will be permitted in case of fire, sickness, pregnant mothers, mothers with young children, and other necessary cases, with the written permission of the Center Manager.

All evacuees shall be in their own living quarters between 10:00 P.M. and 6:00 A.M. Exceptions will be permitted for persons going to and from the nearest lavatory, or when necessary in caring for sick persons. The Center Manager may issue written exceptions in other cases which in his opinion are warranted by circumstances. Evacuees, when assigned to work between the hours of 10:00 p.m. and 6:00 a.m. shall be provided by the Center Manager with a written exemption from this ruling, giving the evacuee's name and address; the duties to which he or she is assigned, and the hours and location of duty.

"I Thank Aki"

Aki left a legacy
to live each day with indomitable courage.
A spirit that could not be destroyed by cancer,
embodied in her heart and soul—PEACE.

Aki's accomplishments:

- honored twice at the White House
- Presidential Award for Excellence in Science Teaching
- appointment by President Carter to the National Advisory Council of Education of Disadvantaged Children
- United Nations Human Rights Award
- Asian American Living Pioneer Award
- Phi Beta Kappa Pathfinder Award
- National Science Honor Roll of Teachers
- Seattle Public Schools Teacher of the Year Award
- Asian Pioneer Award for Peace
- National Japanese American Citizens League

Additional Notes:

President Truman's Committee on Civil Rights stated in a report: "Time is often needed for us to recognize the great miscarriages of justice."

Charles Van Hughes, noted statesman and jurist once warned: "You may think that the Constitution is your security—it is nothing but a piece of paper. You may think that the statutes are your security—they are nothing but words in a book. You may think that elaborate mechanism of government is your security—it is nothing at all, unless you have sound and uncorrupted public opinion to give life to our Constitution, to give vitality to your statues, to make efficient your government machinery."

We are reminded that the sanctity of the Constitution rests with its citizens, and they must be vigilant to assure that the principles on which this country was founded will be honored.

Bibliography:

Bosworth, Allan R.
America's Concentration Camps
1967 New York : W. W. Norton & Company, Inc

Chang, Thelma
I Can Never Forget: Men of the 100th/442nd
1991 Honolulu, HI : Sigi Productions

Duus, Masayo
Unlikely Liberators: The Men of the 100th And 442nd
1987 Honolulu : University of Hawaii Press

Fiset, Louis
Camp Harmony : Seattle's Japanese Americans and the Puyallup Assembly Center
2009 Urbana : University of Illinois Press

Fisher, Anne Reeploeg
Exile of a Race
1987 Seattle: A.R. Fisher

Hanley, James M
A Matter of Honor: A Mémoire
1995 New York: Vantage Press

Hosokawa, Bill
Nisei : the Quiet Americans
1969 New York : William Morrow

Myer, Dillon S., (Dillon Seymour), 1891-1982.
Uprooted Americans : The Japanese Americans and the War Relocation Authority During World War II
1971 Tucson : University of Arizona Press

United States Commission on Wartime Relocation and Internment of Civilians.
Personal Justice Denied
1997 Wash., D.C. : Civil Liberties Public Education Fund; Seattle : University of Washington Press

Weglyn, Michi
Years of Infamy : The Untold Story of America's Concentration Camps
1996 Seattle : University of Washington Press

Photo Credits

Location	Caption	Credit
Cover	*Entrance to the Minidoka concentration camp, aka "Relocation Center," superimposed with an image of first grade students saying the Pledge of Allegiance.*	*Densho: The Japanese American Legacy Project*
Title Page	*Entrance to the Minidoka concentration camp, showing the guard tower and administration buildings.*	*Densho: The Japanese American Legacy Project*
Section I	*The Kato Family* *Front Row: Suma and Aki* *Back Row, Haruotoshi, Fusae, Murako, Haruo, and family friend*	
Section II	*Haruotoshi and Murako Kato, Suma's father and mother - Photo taken on the lawn in front of the Eleanor Apartments building they owned.*	
Section III	*Opposite page:* *Instructions posted in Seattle instructing Japanese Americans how to comply with the evacuation decree.* *Soldier nailing placards containing Civilian Exclusion Order No. 1 and special instructions to all Japanese residents of Bainbridge Island.*	*Densho: The Japanese American Legacy Project* *Courtesy of the Museum of History & Industry*
Section IV	*Muddy conditions around the barracks at the Puyallup Assembly Center, also known as "Camp Harmony." It was constructed on the racetrack of the Puyallup fairgrounds. The Assembly Center was open from April 28 - September 23, 1942.*	*Courtesy of the Museum of History & Industry, Seattle Post-Intelligencer Collection*

Location	Caption	Credit
Section V	Man and woman in front of the camp guard house at the Minidoka concentration camp.	Courtesy of the Wing Luke Museum, the Hatate Collection
Section VI	Japanese American soldiers leaving Minidoka in a covered army truck while internees wait to say goodbye.	Courtesy of the Wing Luke Museum, the Hatate Collection
Section VII	Opposite page top: The Higo Ten-Cent Store, located on Jackson Street, after the evacuation. The Murakamis were able to reopen their store after the war because they were able to pay property taxes while interned.	Courtesy of the Museum of History & Industry
	Opposite page lower left: Issei woman leaving the barracks to shower at the communal washing facility.	Courtesy of the Wing Luke Museum
	Opposite page lower right: The Kato sisters, left to right, Suma, Aki, Fusae.	Courtesy of the Kurose Family Collection
	Top: Internees waiting in line for a meal outside of the mess hall.	Museum of History & Industry, Seattle Post-Intelligencer Collection
	Bottom: Two children playing between barracks in Minidoka concentration camp. (Irene and Hiroshi Ito)	Courtesy of the Wing Luke Museum, the Hatate Collection
Notes	Top: Racial epithet written on a garage in Seattle.	Museum of History & Industry, Seattle Post-Intelligencer Collection
	Bottom: Internees stuffing straw into cloth bags for use as mattresses. (Photo taken at the Colorado River Relocation Center.)	Courtesy of the National Archives and Records Administration

About the Author

SUMA (KATO) YAGI was born in Seattle, Washington in 1927. At the outbreak of WWII, when she was fifteen years old and a freshman at Garfield High School, she and her family were forced to leave their home in Seattle. They were sent to the Puyallup Assembly Center and then to the Minidoka concentration camp in Idaho. At the end of WWII, Suma and her family moved back to Seattle, where she married Takeo Yagi and raised four children. Suma worked for the State Human Rights Commission and then at South Seattle Community College. For more than forty years, Suma remained silent about her experience of being sent to a concentration camp, until she took a writing course and discovered an outlet to tell her stories. She still lives in Seattle and her four children and seven grandchildren all live in the area.

About the Editors

VICTOR YAGI is on one of Suma's four children. He helped Suma assemble her poems and produce this book because the poems taught him what "Camp" meant for his mother and father in a way that history books did not and could not.

FRANCES MCCUE is a poet, writer and Senior Lecturer in the University of Washington English Department. Fifteen years ago, while she was the Founding Director of Richard Hugo House, Frances met Suma and was inspired and moved by her poetry. It's been her honor to assist in the creation of this book.